Eloi Rylan Koios (Ed.)

Senior Status

Eloi Rylan Koios (Ed.)

Senior Status

United States Federal Judge

Tract

Imprint

Publisher:
Tract is a trademark of
International Book Market Service Ltd., 17 Rue Meldrum, Beau Bassin, 1713-01 Mauritius
Email: info@bookmarketservice.com
Website: www.bookmarketservice.com

Published in 2011

Printed in: U.S.A., U.K., Germany. This book was not produced in Mauritius.

ISBN: 978-613-8-94412-6

Contents

Articles

References

Senior_status

Senior status is a form of semi-retirement for United States federal judges, and judges in some state court systems. After federal judges have reached a certain combination of age and years of service on the federal courts, they are allowed to assume senior status. A judge must be at least 65 and have served for 15 years to qualify, with one fewer year of service required for each additional year of age. When that happens, they receive the full salary of a judge but work only part-time. Additionally, senior judges do not occupy seats; instead, their seats become vacant, and the President may appoint new full-time judges to fill their spots. Depending on how heavy a caseload they carry, senior judges remain entitled to maintain a staffed office, including a secretary and one or more law clerks.

Statutory requirements

Senior status is defined by statutory law, specifically 28 U.S.C. § 371 [1]. To be in senior status, §371(e)(1) requires that a judge must be annually certified by the chief judge as having met at least one of the following criteria:

- Having carried, in the preceding calendar year, a caseload involving courtroom participation which is equal to or greater than the amount of similar work which an average judge in active service would perform in three months. §371(e)(1)(a).
- Having performed, in the preceding calendar year, substantial judicial duties not involving courtroom participation, but including settlement efforts, motion decisions, writing opinions in cases that have not been orally argued, and administrative duties for the court to which the justice or judge is assigned. §371(e)(1)(b).
- Having performed substantial administrative duties, either directly relating to the operation of the courts, *or* for a Federal or State governmental entity. §371(e)(1)(d)

In addition, §371(e)(1)(e) provides that a judge not meeting these criteria may still be certified as being in senior status by the Chief Justice anyway, provided that the judge did not meet those criteria "because of a temporary or permanent disability."

Nomenclature

The United States code does not refer to *senior status* in its body text, although the title of 28 U.S.C. § 371 is "Retirement on salary; retirement in senior status."

The term *senior judge* is defined by 28 U.S.C. § 294 [2] to mean an inferior court judge who is in senior status.

Justices of the Supreme Court usually retire rather than taking senior status; a Justice having this status is thereafter referred to as a "retired justice." *Senior judge* is explicitly defined by 28 U.S.C. § 294, also explicitly refers to the assignment of retired justices, making no mention of *senior justice*. When a circuit or district judge on senior status sits on an inferior court case, he or she is referred to as "Senior Judge" in the opinion, while a justice in the same position is referred to as "Justice, Retired."

Assignment

The rules governing assignment of senior judges are also defined by statutory law, specifically 28 U.S.C. § 294 [2]. In essence, under normal conditions, the chief judge or judicial council of a circuit may assign a senior judge belonging to that circuit to perform any duty within the circuit that the judge is willing and able to perform. This contains the implication that a senior district judge could be assigned to an appellate case or a circuit judge could be assigned to preside over a trial. For courts that do not fall within a circuit, such as the United States Court of International Trade, the chief judge of that court can assign a senior judge of that court to perform any duty within the circuit that the judge is willing and able to perform.

In special cases, the Chief Justice can assign a senior judge to any court. This, however, requires that a certification of necessity be issued by the appropriate supervisor of the court. For a circuit or district court, this supervisor is either the chief judge or the circuit justice of the circuit. For any other court, this supervisor is the chief judge of the court.

Retired justices can be assigned to any court (except the Supreme Court) the justice is willing to accept. Theoretically, a retired justice could also be assigned to act as Circuit Justice for a circuit, but this has never occurred.

History

In 1919, Congress created the senior status option for inferior court judges. Before the senior status option was created, a judge who reached the age of seventy with at least ten years of service as a federal judge was allowed to retire and receive a pension for the rest of his life; afterwards, a judge who qualified for retirement could instead assume senior status. John Wesley Warrington became the first federal judge to exercise this option on October 6, 1919. At that time, Warrington had been on the bench for ten years and six months, and was 75 years old.

In 1937, the option was extended to Supreme Court justices, although justices so electing are generally referred to as "retired" justices rather than as on senior status. A senior justice is essentially an at-large senior judge, able to be assigned to any inferior federal court by the Chief Justice, but receiving the salary of a retired justice. However, a retired justice no longer participates in the work of the Supreme Court itself.

In 1954, Congress modified entry requirements for the senior status option. Federal judges or justices could still assume senior status at seventy with ten years of service, but they could also assume senior status at 65 with fifteen years of service. In 1984, the requirements were further modified to what is often called the "Rule of 80": once a judge or justice reached age 65, any combination of years of age and years of service on the federal bench which totaled to eighty entitled the judge to assume senior status.

Senior status was not originally known as such. In 1919, when the senior status option was created, a judge who had assumed what we now call "senior status" was referred to as a "retired judge". The title of "senior judge" was instead used to refer to the active judge with the most seniority in a given court; after 1948, this notion was formalized and modified under the new title of "chief judge". In 1958, the term "senior judge" was given its current meaning of a judge who had assumed senior status.

A few states have a similar system for judges. These include Iowa, for judges on the Iowa Court of Appeals, Pennsylvania and Virginia, for Justices of the Virginia Supreme Court.

Constitutionality

Some authors have suggested that senior status may be unconstitutional.[3]

Notes

[1] http://www.law.cornell.edu/uscode/28/371.html

[2] http://www.law.cornell.edu/uscode/28/294.html

[3] Stras, David R. and Scott, Ryan W. (2007). "Are Senior Judges Unconstitutional?" (http://papers.ssrn.com/sol3/papers.cfm?abstract_id=886711). *Cornell Law Review* **92**. .

References

- 28 U.S.C. § 294 (http://www.law.cornell.edu/uscode/html/uscode28/usc_sec_28_00000294----000-.html) and 28 U.S.C. § 371 (http://www.law.cornell.edu/uscode/html/uscode28/usc_sec_28_00000371----000-.html) – statutory authorization and criterion for senior status.

- "About the Federal Judges Biographical Database" (http://web.archive.org/web/20060311101417/http://www.fjc.gov/history/home.nsf/page/about_judges_db). *Official website of the Federal Judicial Center*. Archived from the original (http://www.fjc.gov/history/home.nsf/page/about_judges_db) on March 11, 2006. Retrieved September 12, 2005.
- "How One Mistake Leads To Another: A Research Note" (http://web.archive.org/web/20050407225511/http://polmeth.wustl.edu/polanalysis/vol/12/ward.doc) (Word document, 89 kB). *Political Analysis*. Archived from the original (http://polmeth.wustl.edu/polanalysis/vol/12/ward.doc) on April 7, 2005. Retrieved May 25, 2005.

United_States_federal_judge

In the United States, the title of **federal judge** usually means a judge appointed by the President of the United States and confirmed by the United States Senate in accordance with Article II of the United States Constitution.

In addition to the Supreme Court of the United States, whose existence and some aspects of whose jurisdiction are beyond the constitutional power of Congress to alter, acts of Congress have established 13 courts of appeals (also called "circuit courts") with appellate jurisdiction over different regions of the United States, and 94 United States district courts. Every judge appointed to such a court falls within the category of federal judges. These include the Chief Justice and Associate Justices of the Supreme Court, Circuit Judges of the courts of appeals, and district judges of the United States district courts. In addition, judges of the Court of International Trade are appointed pursuant to Article III.

Other judges serving in the federal courts, including magistrate judges and bankruptcy judges, are also sometimes referred to as "federal judges"; however, they are not appointed pursuant to the procedures designated in Article III. The distinction is sometimes expressed by saying that they are not "Article III judges," because the power of these other kinds of federal judges does not derive from Article III of the U.S. Constitution. See Article I and Article III tribunals.

Tenure and salary

"Article III federal judges" (as opposed to judges of some courts with special jurisdictions) serve "during good behavior" (often paraphrased as appointed "for life"). Judges hold their seats until they resign, die, or are removed from office. Although the legal orthodoxy is that judges cannot be removed from office except by impeachment by the House of Representatives followed by conviction by the Senate, several legal scholars, including William Rehnquist, Saikrishna Prakash and Steven D. Smith, have argued that the Good Behaviour Clause may, in theory, permit removal by way of a writ of *scire facias* filed before a federal court, without resort to impeachment.

Since the impeachment process requires a trial by the United States Senate, and since the constitutional provision concerning federal judges' tenure cannot be changed without the ratifications of three-fourths of the states, federal judges have perhaps the best job security available in the United States. Moreover, the Constitution forbids Congress to diminish a federal judge's salary. Twentieth-century experience suggests that Congress is generally unwilling to take time out of its busy schedule to impeach and try a federal judge until, after criminal conviction, he or she is already in prison and still drawing a salary, which cannot otherwise be taken away (see *Nixon v. United States,* a key Supreme Court case about Congress's discretion in impeaching and trying federal judges).

As of January 2008, federal district judges were paid $169,300 a year, circuit judges $179,500, Associate Justices of the Supreme Court $208,100 and the Chief Justice of the United States $217,400. All were permitted to earn a maximum of an additional $21,000 a year for teaching.[1]

Chief Justice John Roberts has repeatedly pleaded for an increase in judicial pay, calling the situation a "constitutional crisis." The problem is that the most talented associates at the largest U.S. law firms with judicial clerkship experience (in other words, the attorneys most qualified to become the next generation of federal judges) already earn as much as a federal judge in their *first year* as full-time associates. Thus, when those attorneys eventually become experienced partners and reach the stage in life where one would normally consider switching to public service, their interest in joining the judiciary is tempered by the prospect of a giant pay cut back to what they were making 10 to 20 years earlier (adjusted for inflation). One way for attorneys to soften the financial blow is to spend only a few years on the bench and then return to private practice or go into private arbitration, but such turnover creates a risk of a revolving door judiciary subject to regulatory capture.

Thus, Chief Justice Roberts has warned that "judges are no longer drawn primarily from among the best lawyers in the practicing bar" and "If judicial appointment ceases to be the capstone of a distinguished career and instead becomes a stepping stone to a lucrative position in private practice, the Framers' goal of a truly independent judiciary will be placed in serious jeopardy."[2] Naturally, the other alternative to raising judicial pay would be to impose wage controls for *all* attorneys, but that would be a political nonstarter. Historically, wartime experiments with emergency wage controls had highly negative effects upon the U.S. economy.

Retirement

Once a Judge meets age and service requirements he may retire and will then earn his final salary for the remainder of his life, plus cost of living increases. The "Rule of 80" is the commonly used shorthand for the age and service requirement for a judge to retire, or assume senior status, as set forth in Title 28 of the US. Code, Section 371(c). Beginning at age 65, a judge may retire at his current salary, or take senior status, after performing 15 years of active service as an Article III judge (65 + 15 = 80). A sliding scale of increasing age and decreasing service (66 + 14, 67 + 13, 68 + 12, 69 + 11) results in eligibility for retirement compensation at age 70 with a minimum of 10 years of service (70 + 10 = 80).[3] [4] [5]

Under section 376 a survivor's annuity to benefit the widow, widower or minor child of the Judge may be purchased via a deduction of 2.2% to 3.5% from the retirement benefit.[6]

Number of judges

The total number of active federal judges is constantly in flux, for two reasons. First, judges retire or die, and a lapse of time usually occurs before new judges are appointed to fill those positions. Second, from time to time Congress will increase (or, less frequently, decrease) the number of federal judgeships in a particular judicial district, usually in response to shifting population numbers or a changing workload in that district.

As of January 2009, a total of 3,168 individuals had been appointed to federal judgeships, including 2,645 district court judges, 687 courts of appeals judges, 50 judges to the now-extinct circuit courts, and the 9 Supreme Court justices. This adds up to 3,492 total appointments; a substantial number of appellate judges (including Supreme Court justices) had previously served on the lower court bench.[7]

There are currently 874 authorized Article III judgeships: nine on the Supreme Court, 179 on the courts of appeals, 9 on the court of international trade and 677 for the district courts.[8] Although the number of Supreme Court Justices has remained the same for well over a century, the number of court of appeals judges has more than doubled since 1950, and the number of district court judges has increased more than three times in that period.[7]

Non-Article III judges

Unlike the judges of Article III courts, non-Article III judges are appointed for specified terms of office. Examples include United States magistrate judges and judges of the United States bankruptcy courts, United States Tax Court, United States Court of Federal Claims, and United States territorial courts.

See also

- Federal judicial appointment history
- List of United States federal judges by longevity of service

References

[1] Senate (http://www.senate.gov/reference/resources/pdf/RL33245.pdf)
[2] 2006 Year-End Report on the Federal Judiciary (http://www.supremecourt.gov/publicinfo/year-end/2006year-endreport.pdf)
[3] http://www.law.cornell.edu/uscode/html/uscode28/usc_sec_28_00000371----000-.html USC Title 28 Section 371
[4] http://www.uscourts.gov/Common/FAQS.aspx#FederalJudges US Courts.COM FAQs on Federal Judges
[5] http://vlex.com/vid/retirement-salary-senior-status-19212714 28 USC 371 – Sec. 371 Retirement – Historical And Revision Notes
[6] http://www.law.cornell.edu/uscode/html/uscode28/usc_sec_28_00000376----000-.html 28 USC 471
[7] Federal Judicial Center (http://www.fjc.gov/history/home.nsf).
[8] www.uscourts.gov (http://www.uscourts.gov/JudgesAndJudgeships/FederalJudgeships.aspx)

- Saikrishna Prakash & Steven D. Smith, *How To Remove a Federal Judge,* 116 Yale L.J. 72 (2006).

External links

- U.S. Courts FAQ (http://www.uscourts.gov/faq.html)
- Judicial Financial Disclosure Reports (http://www.judicialwatch.org/jfd.shtml)

United_States_federal_courts

The **United States federal courts** make up the judiciary branch of federal government of the United States organized under the United States Constitution and laws of the federal government.

Categories

The courts are one of the three coequal branches of the federal government, and include:

Highest court

- Court of last resort:
  - Supreme Court of the United States (which primarily has appellate jurisdiction but also has original jurisdiction over a very narrow range of cases)

Appellate courts

- Courts with geographic-based appellate jurisdiction:
  - The eleven numbered United States courts of appeals
  - The United States Courts of Appeals for the District of Columbia
- Courts with appellate jurisdiction over specific subject matter:
  - United States Court of Appeals for Veterans Claims
  - United States Court of Appeals for the Armed Forces
  - United States Court of Appeals for the Federal Circuit
  - United States Foreign Intelligence Surveillance Court of Review

Original jurisdiction

- General trial courts:
  - United States district courts
- Courts with original jurisdiction over specific subject matter:
  - United States Alien Terrorist Removal Court[1]
  - United States bankruptcy courts
  - United States Court of Federal Claims
  - United States Court of International Trade
  - United States Court of Private Land Claims (1891-1904)
  - United States Foreign Intelligence Surveillance Court
  - United States Tax Court

While federal courts are generally created by the United States Congress under the constitutional power described in Article III, many of the specialized courts are created under the authority granted in Article I. Greater power is vested in Article III courts because they are independent of Congress, the President, and the political process.

Article III requires the establishment of a Supreme Court and permits the Congress to create other federal courts, and place limitations on their jurisdiction. In theory, Congress could eliminate the entire federal judiciary except for the Supreme Court, although the 1st Congress established a system of lower federal courts through the Judiciary Act of 1789.

Levels of U.S. federal courts

Civil procedure in the United States

• *Federal Rules of Civil Procedure*
• *Doctrines of civil procedure*
• Jurisdiction
• Venue
• Pleadings and motions
• Pleadings
  • Service of process
  • Complaint
  • Answer
  • Counterclaim
  • Crossclaim
• Pre-trial procedure
  • Discovery
  • Interrogatories
  • Depositions
  • Request for Admissions
  • Request for Production
• Resolution without trial
  • Default judgment
  • Summary judgment
  • Voluntary dismissal
  • Involuntary dismissal
  • Settlement
• Trial
  • Parties
  • Jury
  • Burden of proof
  • Judgment
• Appeal
  • Mandamus
  • Certiorari

The United States district courts are the general federal trial courts, although in many cases Congress has passed statutes which divert original jurisdiction to the above-mentioned specialized courts or to administrative law judges (ALJs). In such cases, the district courts have jurisdiction to hear appeals from such lower bodies.

The United States courts of appeals are the federal intermediate appellate courts. They operate under a system of mandatory review which means they *must* hear all appeals of right from the lower courts.

The Supreme Court of the United States is the supreme court (court of last resort). It generally is an appellate court that operates under discretionary review; meaning that the Court, through granting of writs of certiorari, can choose which cases to hear. There is generally no right of appeal to the Supreme Court. In a few situations (like lawsuits between state governments or some cases between the federal government and a state) it sits as a court of original jurisdiction. Such matters are generally referred to a designated individual (usually a sitting or retired judge or well-respected attorney) to sit as a special master and report to the Court with recommendations.

Related organizations

- The Judicial Conference of the United States is the policymaking body of the U.S. federal courts. The Conference is responsible for creating and revising federal procedural rules pursuant to the Rules Enabling Act.
- The Judicial Panel on Multidistrict Litigation transfers and consolidates cases in multiple judicial districts that share common factual issues.
- The United States Marshals Service is responsible for providing protection for the federal judiciary and transporting federal prisoners.
- The Supreme Court Police provide security for the Supreme Court building.

Limitations on U.S. federal courts

The Supreme Court has interpreted the Constitution as placing some additional restrictions on the federal courts. For example, the doctrines of mootness, ripeness, and standing prohibit district courts from issuing advisory opinions. Other doctrines, such as the abstention doctrine and the *Rooker-Feldman* doctrine limit the power of lower federal courts to disturb rulings made by state courts. The *Erie* doctrine requires federal courts to apply substantive state law to claims arising from state law (which may be heard in federal courts under supplemental or diversity jurisdiction). In difficult cases, the federal courts must either guess as to how a court of that state would decide the issue or "certify" the issue to a state court if the state has provided for such a procedure.

Notably, the only federal court that can issue proclamations of federal law that bind state courts is the Supreme Court itself. Decisions of the lower federal courts on issues of federal law are persuasive but not binding authority in the states in which those federal courts sit.[2]

Study of U.S. federal courts

Most U.S. law schools offer an elective course that focuses specifically on the powers and limitations of U.S. federal courts, with coverage of topics such as justiciability, abstention doctrines, the abrogation doctrine, and habeas corpus.

See also

- Article I and Article III tribunals
- CM/ECF (Case Management/Electronic Case Files)
- Courts of the United States (outline of all state and federal courts in the United States)
- Federal Rules of Civil Procedure
- State court (United States)
- State supreme court
- Uniformity and jurisdiction in U.S. federal court tax decisions
- United States Marshals Service

References

[1] 8 U.S.C. § 1531 (http://www.law.cornell.edu/uscode/8/1531.html) *et seq.*

[2] *People v. Leonard*, 40 Cal. 4th 1370, 1416 (http://online.ceb.com/calcases/C4/40C4t1370.htm) (2007) (Ninth Circuit decisions on federal law do not bind Supreme Court of California).

External links

- The Federal Judiciary (official U.S. government site) (http://www.uscourts.gov/)
- United States Federal Courts @ OpenJurist (http://openjurist.org/us-court)
- Federal Court Concepts, Georgia Tech (http://www.catea.org/grade/legal/)
- Federal District Court Case Filings (http://dockets.justia.com/)
- Creating the Federal Judicial System (http://www.fjc.gov/public/pdf.nsf/lookup/creating.pdf/$File/creating.pdf) (PDF)
- History of the Courts of the Federal Judiciary (http://www.fjc.gov/history/home.nsf)
- CourtWEB, Online Federal Court Opinions Information System (http://courtweb.pamd.uscourts.gov/courtweb/CourtWeb.aspx)

Law_clerk

A **law clerk** or a **judicial clerk** is a person who provides assistance to a judge in researching issues before the court and in writing opinions. Law clerks are *not* court clerks or courtroom deputies, who are administrative staff for the court. Most law clerks are recent law school graduates who performed at or near the top of their class. Various studies have shown clerks to be influential in the formation of case law through their influence on judges' decisions. Working as a law clerk generally opens up career opportunities.

While there has been relatively little inquiry comparing clerks across nations, some research has been done comparing clerkship practices in the U.S. with non-U.S. courts. Still, in some countries the position of law clerk does not exist. But in many nations clerk-duties are performed by permanent staff attorneys or junior apprentice-like judges, such as those that sit on France's Conseil d'État. In English Courts, they are known as Judicial Assistants. The permanent staff attorneys, or clerks—called *Referendaires* at the European Court of Justice provide one point of comparison to American clerks. Australian, Canadian, Swedish and Brazilian practices can also help illuminate the similarities and differences across nations.

Australia

In Australia, the position of law clerk is known either as "Associate" (in the High Court of Australia, the Federal Court of Australia and most State Supreme Courts) or "Tipstaff" (in the Supreme Court of New South Wales). The positions usually run for one-year, although they are sometimes extended to two years (this is more common in the Supreme Courts).

The duties of associates and tipstaves can include research, reviewing draft judgments and providing feedback or criticism to the judge, reading and summarising court materials, attending to the judge in court, and also assisting with chambers, administrative or personal tasks. On occasion, some associates and tipstaves are asked to write draft judgments, or parts of judgments. However, these duties can vary between different courts, and also depend on the individual judge.

In the High Court, each of the seven High Court judges has two associates at any given time. Usually, one associate is based permanently in Canberra, the capital of Australia and the seat of the Court, and one travels with the judge when the Court is on circuit to the other capital cities of Australia. The traveling associate in practice is usually based in the judge's home city. Associateships at the High Court are extremely competitive and usually go to the top graduates from the top law schools of Australia. Each judge has his or her own method for interviewing and appointing associates. Previous associates have written that the nature of the associate's role is different from that of a law clerk in the United States.[1]

The judges of the Federal Court and the Supreme Courts of each State (and Territory) have one associate each. These positions are also very competitive.

There are also research positions available at the superior courts in Australia and the High Court. These positions are similarly staffed by recent law graduates and young lawyers.

Canada

Most Canadian courts accept applications for judicial clerkships from graduating law students or experienced lawyers who have already been called to the Bar in Canada or abroad (typically in the United States or the United Kingdom). Most provincial superior and appellate courts hire at least one clerk for each judge. Typically students in their last two years of law school are eligible to apply for these positions, but increasingly, experienced practicing lawyers are also considered for these positions. The term typically lasts a year and generally fulfills the articling requirement for provincial law societies, which qualifies a person to become a practicing lawyer in a Canadian jurisdiction.

The most prestigious clerkship available is with the country's highest court, the Supreme Court of Canada, followed by the Courts of Appeal of the three most populous provinces: Ontario Court of Appeal, Quebec Court of Appeal, and British Columbia Court of Appeal. Each Justice of the Supreme Court hires three clerks for a one-year period.[2] The Court of Appeal for Ontario selects 17 law clerks, who serve either one or two of the 24 Justices.[3] The Quebec Court of Appeal usually hires a similar number of law clerks for both Montreal and Quebec City, but is unusual among Canadian courts in having a formal clerkship program for law students in addition to law graduates. Successful candidates for all clerkships are usually selected based on a distinguished academic record, academic recommendations, strong research and writing skills and interviews with judges. For both the Supreme Court of Canada and the Quebec Court of Appeal, being able to work in both English and French is strongly preferred.[4] Many law clerks have gone on to become leaders of the profession. For example, the Hon. Mr. Justice Jean Cote of the Alberta Court of Appeal was one of the very first Supreme Court law clerks, serving as a clerk in the program's inaugural year (1967). Similarly, the Hon. Madam Justice Louise Arbour, formerly of the Supreme Court of Canada, the International Criminal Tribunal for Rwanda and the International Criminal Tribunal for the former Yugoslavia and former UN High Commissioner for Human Rights, also served as a law clerk in the early years of the program. Meanwhile, the Hon. Madam Justice Andromache Karakatsanis and the Hon. Madam Justice Kathryn N. Feldman of the Ontario Court of Appeal were formerly law clerks at the same court.

In Canada, a law clerk is also the chief legal counsel to the Senate, the House of Commons and some provincial or territorial legislative assemblies.

England and Wales

In England and Wales, law clerks are called Judicial Assistants. It is possible to be a Judicial Assistant at the Court of Appeal and at the UK Supreme Court (formerly the Appellate Committee of the House of Lords). Only Supreme Court Judicial Assistants are appointed for a full-time, one year fixed term appointment. Since 2006 they have taken part in a week long exchange in Washington DC at the U.S. Supreme Court due to a friendship between Justice Antonin Scalia and Lord Rodger of Earlsferry.

European Court of Justice

Sally Kenney's article on clerks, or *Référendaires*, on the European Court of Justice (ECJ) provides one detailed point of comparison (2000). There are some major differences between ECJ clerks and their American counterparts, largely because of the way the ECJ is structured[5] . One key difference is that ECJ clerks, while hired by individual judges, serve long tenures as opposed to the one-year-clerkship norm at the U.S. Supreme Court. This gives ECJ clerks considerable expertise and power. Because ECJ judges serve six-year renewable terms and do not issue individual opinions, the most important role of ECJ clerks is to facilitate uniformity and continuity across chambers, member-states, and over time.

Furthermore, this role is heightened because the European Union is composed of very different nations with disparate legal systems. Kenney found that ECJ clerks provide legal and linguistic expertise (all opinions are issued in French), ease the workload of their members, participate in oral and written interactions between chambers, and provide continuity as members rapidly change. While Kenney concludes that they have more power than their counterparts on the U.S. Supreme Court, ECJ clerks act as agents for their principals—judges—and are not the puppeteers that critics suggest.

France

In France law clerks are called assistants de justice. They typically go through a competitive nomination and interview process to get accepted as law clerks. Most French courts accept applications for judicial clerkships from graduating law students. Students in their last year of law school are eligible to apply, although most law clerks are Ph.D. candidates in Law or candidates for a French competitive entrance exam such as the bar exam, French National School for the Judiciary, French National School of Public Finances, or French National School of Court Clerks.

Law clerks are hired for two years renewable twice.[6] Depending on credentials and curriculum they can be assigned to the bench (magistrat du siège) or the prosecution (parquet or parquet général).

The work of a law clerk entails assisting the judges with writing verdicts and decisions and conducting legal inquiries and research.

The most prestigious clerkships available in France are before the courts of appeals, which review decisions of lower courts.

The largest appeal courts in France are in Paris,[7] Versailles,[8] Aix-en-Provence,[9] and Rennes.[10]

A similar system exists in the administrative courts.[11]

Germany

In Germany, there are two different kinds of law clerks.

Students of law who, after law school, have passed the first of two required examinations join the *Referendariat*, a time of two years consisting of a series of clerkships: for a civil law judge, a criminal law judge or a prosecutor, a government office and finally at a law firm.

In the Federal Supreme Courts (see Judiciary of Germany) and the office of the Federal Prosecutor General, the duties of law clerks are performed by *wissenschaftliche Mitarbeiter* (German for "scientific assistant"). With few exceptions, they are lower court judges or civil servants, assigned for a period of three years to the respective Federal Court, and their clerkships serve as a qualification for a higher judgeship. However, some justices of the Federal Constitutional Court (who have the right to select their *wissenschaftliche Mitarbeiter* personally) prefer clerks from outside the courts or the civil service, especially those who are or were professors of law and who often hire people from academia (sometimes even young law professors). The clerks of the Federal Constitutional Court are deemed very influential and are therefore dubbed the (unofficial) *Dritter Senat* ("Third Senate") as opposed to the two official "senates" of 8 justices each which form the court.

India

In India law graduates from the country's best law schools go through a competitive nomination and interview process to get accepted as law clerks. The Supreme Court of India and several High Courts of India offer paid law clerkships that are considered very prestigious. These clerkships usually last a year and may be extended at the discretion of individual judges.

The Registry of the Supreme Court of India invites applications in January each year for 'law clerk-cum research assistant' positions. The selected applicants are then allocated to work under the sitting judges of the Supreme Court. Usually, one 'law clerk' is assigned to each judge for an year, though some justices are known to engage two or more law clerks at a time. The 'law clerks' usually begin their one-year service period in July each year, soon after the completion of the LL.B. degree, though there have been instances of 'law clerks' serving after having accumulated some work experience.

For the 2010-11 session each judicial clerk at the Supreme Court was paid Rs 25,000 a month, which may be increased further in the next year. In 2009-2010 each law clerk at the Supreme Court of India was being paid Rs. 20,000 per month.[12]

In addition to this, students from law colleges all over the country are given the opportunity to act as 'legal trainees' under Supreme Court judges during their vacation periods. The institution of law clerks is still a recent development in the context of the Indian judiciary. Anecdotal references indicate that some justices are hesitant to rely on 'law clerks' on account of concerns with confidentiality, especially in politically sensitive disputes. However, their services are heavily relied on to go through the written submissions in order to prepare for the preliminary hearings that are held to decide whether a case should be admitted for a regular hearing on merits. In recent years, the contributions of law clerks to research for judicial opinions has become increasingly evident on account of increasing references to foreign precedents and academic writings.

Ireland

In Ireland Judicial Fellows provide support to judges of the High Court comparable to that provided to judges of the Federal Courts of the United States, the Courts of Australia and the European Courts in Luxembourg and Strasbourg. During 2008, ten judicial fellowships were awarded for a two year period to law graduates who are also qualified to practise as barristers or solicitors. They were assigned by the President of the High Court to work directly with one or two judges whose major commitment is to judicial review, chancery, commercial, asylum and competition lists in the High Court.[13]

Mexico

In Mexico, duties conferred to law clerks in some common law countries are charged in a person called "Secretario de Acuerdos", for lower courts and, "Secretario de Estudio y Cuenta" for higher court: "Suprema Corte de Justicia de la Nación". Secretario de Acuerdo's main activities are: conduct the public hearings, writing veredicts, order to execute sentences, and providing general assistance to Judges.

New Zealand

Law clerks are referred to as judge's clerks in the Supreme Court, Court of Appeal and High Courts. In the District Court, they are called research counsels. It is a fixed term position of 2 years.

Philippines

In the Supreme Court of the Philippines and the Philippine Court of Appeals, recent law graduates and young lawyers can apply for a position as a "Court Attorney" to a Justice. This position basically corresponds to what is called a "law clerk" at the Supreme Court of the United States. Each of the 15 Supreme Court justices has 5 to 10 court attorneys at any given time. Court attorneys at the Supreme Court of the Philippines are co-terminus with their justices. Some stay for one year or less, others stay for as long as their respective justice serves the Court. Previous court attorneys have become notable Justices themselves e.g. Justice Vicente V. Mendoza, Justice Antonio Abad etc. or have gone to hold important positions in the court such as Court Administrators or Deputy Court Administrators. Many of them have gone on to successful legal practice, in business, or in the academe. The position is an extremely difficult one to get accepted to because aside from the competence requirement, there is also the character requirement that differ from one Justice to another. The position is basically a confidential one and the lawyer must enjoy the Justice's trust. Each justice has his or her own method for interviewing and appointing court attorneys.

Singapore

In Singapore, top law graduates from the National University of Singapore and reputable foreign universities, usually only those obtaining first class honours, are invited to join the Supreme Court as Justices' Law Clerks. The Supreme Court comprises the High Court and the Court of Appeal, which is the final court of appeal in Singapore. Upon accepting appointment, Justices' Law Clerks are appointed for a term of one and a half years, with a possible 6 month extension. During their term, the law clerks are given the opportunity to work with both the judges of the High Court as well as the Judges of the Appeal and the Chief Justice. After their term, the law clerks have the option of joining the permanent establishment of the Singapore Legal Service. If they take up this option, they will be posted to other branches of the Singapore Legal Service, for example as Deputy Public Prosecutors at the Attorney's General Chambers or as Assistant Registrars in the Supreme Court Registry. Many Justice's Law Clerks choose to join private firms after their stint (and several have recently achieved the title of Senior Counsel), while others have chosen a path in academia.

The Netherlands

Law clerks of the Supreme Court of the Netherlands are independent researchers. Applicants are recruited from the top law firms and universities. For most, it is a highly prestigious second job. Law clerks typically work at the Surpreme Court for six years.

Sweden

After successfully obtaining the Swedish law degree called Candidate of Law one can apply for a position as a law clerk ("notarie" in Swedish) either in the Administrative Courts (förvaltningsrätt)[14] or in the General Courts (tingsrätt) [15]. Applicants are rated according to their accumulated points, which are calculated mainly by grades. Higher grades giving higher scores and the one with the highest score applying to any given spot is accepted. One applies to the Swedish Court Agency (Domstolsverket) about six times a year, which calculates the scores and apportions the applicants. The Courts in the bigger cities naturally tends to be most popular, thereby needing the highest scores even if they also have most law clerk positions.

The ratio is about one law clerk per judge, and the clerk switch judge after a time, usually three months. The rationale being that working for different judges broadens the scope of learning.

The term as law clerk is two years, after which the law clerk may opt to apply to the Court of Appeals in the Administrative system or the General system ("kammarrätt" or "hovrätt") and continue on the path that traditionally leads to Judge, or leave the Court system for another career. Having completed the two years is considered qualifying and may open up career opportunities otherwise closed.

The work as a law clerk mainly entails assisting the judges with writing verdicts and decisions, keeping the records during trials and conducting legal inquirys. After about six months the law clerk is trusted with deciding simpler non-disputed issues by himself (such as registering prenuptials or granting adoptions). After about a year the law clerk is entrusted with judging simpler criminal and civil law cases by himself (in General Courts), such as petty theft or a civil case involving low sums of money.

United States

Among the most prestigious clerkships are those with the United States Supreme Court, the United States courts of appeals, certain United States district courts, specialized courts such as the United States Tax Court and the Delaware Court of Chancery, and state supreme courts. Some U.S. district courts provide particularly useful experience for law clerks pursuing specific fields. The Southern District of New York deals with a heightened volume of high-profile commercial litigation, while the District of Columbia hears many high-profile disputes involving the federal government. Similarly, the United States Tax Court specializes in adjudicating disputes over federal income tax, and the Delaware Court of Chancery hears a substantial volume of corporate and shareholder derivative actions.

Qualifications

Most law clerks are recent law school graduates who performed at or near the top of their class. Federal judges, especially those at the appellate level, often require that applicants for law clerk positions have experience with law review or moot court in law school. As such, the law clerk application process is highly competitive, with most federal judges receiving hundreds of applications for only one or two open positions in any given year. State-level trial court judges are less likely to get law clerks with the highest credentials because the majority of such candidates are hired by federal judges or state appellate judges.[16]

Supreme Court Justice Byron White previously served as a law clerk to Chief Justice Frederick M. Vinson.

Because of the selection criteria, many notable legal figures, professors, and judges were initially law clerks.

Six Supreme Court justices previously clerked for other Supreme Court justices: Byron White clerked for Frederick M. Vinson, John Paul Stevens clerked for Wiley Rutledge, Stephen Breyer clerked for Arthur Goldberg, William H. Rehnquist clerked for Robert H. Jackson, John G. Roberts, Jr. clerked for William H. Rehnquist, and Elena Kagan clerked for Thurgood Marshall.

Some judges seek to hire law clerks who not only have excelled academically but also share the judge's ideological orientation. However, this occurs mostly at the level of some state supreme courts and the United States Supreme Court. Law clerks can have a great deal of influence on the judges with whom they work.

Upon completing a judicial clerkship, a law clerk often becomes very marketable to elite law firms. However, some law clerks decide they enjoy the position so much they continue to serve the judge as a law clerk in a permanent capacity.

Federal clerkships

A clerkship with a federal judge is one of the most highly-sought positions in the legal field. Some federal judges receive thousands of applications for a single position, and even the least sought-after federal clerkships will be applied to by at least 50 people. Successful candidates tend to be very high in their class, with most being members of their law school's law review or other journal or moot court team. Such clerkships are generally seen as more prestigious than those with state judges.

Almost all federal judges have at least one law clerk; many have two or more. Associate Justices of the U.S. Supreme Court are allowed four clerks. Although the Chief Justice is allowed to hire five clerks, Chief Justice Rehnquist hired only three per year, and Chief Justice Roberts usually hires only four. Generally, law clerks serve a term of one to two years; however, some federal judges hire a permanent law clerk. Such judges usually have one permanent law clerk and one or two law clerks who serve on a term basis.

The most prestigious clerkship is one with a U.S. Supreme Court Justice; there are only 36 of these positions available every year. However, in recent times securing a federal court of appeals clerkship with a federal judge has been a prerequisite to clerking on the Supreme Court. The next most prestigious place to clerk is at one of the U.S. courts of appeals. Further, clerkships with a court of appeals judge such as J. Michael Luttig who sent many clerks on to the Supreme Court, often called feeder judges, (e.g., Alex Kozinski, J. Harvie Wilkinson III, Merrick Garland) are especially difficult to obtain. Luttig, before his retirement, was the leading "feeder" judge on the U.S. Court of Appeals, with virtually all of his law clerks having gone on to clerk with conservative justices on the Supreme Court,[17] a total of 40 with 33 clerking for either Justice Thomas or Justice Scalia. This reflects the increasing polarization of the court with both liberal and conservative judges hiring clerks who reflect their ideological orientation.[18]

Generally, the third most sought after clerkship is one with a United States District Court judge; like the Court of Appeals, some U.S. District Courts are more sought after than others due to the district's popular location. There are also federal clerkships with lower level trial-court judges, like magistrate judges (who are hired by district court judges), United States Tax Court Special Trial judges (who are supervised by United States Tax Court judges), or bankruptcy judges, whose cases are appealable to United States district court.

Former federal law clerks are generally highly sought by large firms. Firms believe that such individuals have excellent legal research and writing skills, and a strong command of the Federal Rules of Civil Procedure and Federal Rules of Criminal Procedure. Firms are even more interested in a former law clerk if the firm generally appears before the clerk's former judge. The interest in former law clerks is seen by the fact that most large firms have a special hiring process for former clerks, and often pay such individuals large signing bonuses.

Generally interested candidates apply for federal clerkships roughly a year before the clerkship begins, meaning that law students formally apply early in the fall of their third year. The federal clerkship application process has also largely been streamlined by the National Federal Judges Law Clerk Hiring Plan and the OSCAR system, an online database in which federal judges post upcoming vacancies (although not all federal judges use this system). The National Federal Judges Law Clerk Hiring Plan sets dates for when federal judges may receive applications, and when they may contact, interview, and hire law clerks. Generally, judges begin looking at applications in the early fall (in 2007 it was Tuesday, September 4), with contact and interviews happening a few weeks later.[19] These dates only apply to the hiring of matriculating third-year law students; practicing attorneys may apply earlier. Moreover, while many judges adhere to the National Federal Judges Law Clerk Hiring Plan's schedule, many do not follow the plan and interview and hire law students over the summer. The Supreme Court does not follow this timetable.

As a result of the extreme competition—both by the judges to get the best candidates and by candidates to get the best clerkships—the pace of the hiring is extremely quick. It is not unknown for federal judges to offer a candidate a clerkship at the conclusion of a first interview, and require that the candidate provide an immediate answer. Such job offers have come to be known as "exploding offers." Some have likened the process to land runs or feeding frenzies. While a few federal clerkships come available after September, most federal judges complete their hiring before the end of October.

Some scholars and practitioners have questioned the lack of a federal congressional clerkship program. One study found that few top law school graduates have or will take seriously the process of being a legislative aide to gain practical skills after graduation.[20] Instead, recent law school graduates opt for judicial clerkships leaving few in the legal field with practical legislative experience.

State clerkships

A clerkship in a state appellate court generally resembles a federal appellate court clerkship, although the position title is often "staff attorney," and state appellate clerkships are usually less competitive and less prestigious than federal clerkships. The position is more likely to be filled with a more experienced attorney on a long-term basis.

History

According to James Chace,[21] Oliver Wendell Holmes, Jr. and Louis Brandeis were the first Supreme Court justices to use recent law school graduates as clerks, rather than hiring a "stenographer-secretary."

Exceptions

The Supreme Court of California and the various districts of the California Court of Appeal have generally avoided using law clerks since the late 1980s.[22]

Instead, California has largely switched to using permanent staff attorneys at all levels of the judiciary; a few judges do use law clerks, but they are quite rare. For example, the Supreme Court of California has over 85 staff attorneys, of whom about half are attached to particular justices and the rest are shared as a central staff. The California system has been heavily criticized for denying young attorneys the chance to gain experience, and low turnover has resulted in a lack of ethnic and gender diversity among the staff attorneys.[22] But most California judges prefer staff attorneys because it avoids the problem of having to bring new law clerks up to speed on pending complex cases, particularly those involving the death penalty.[22]

See also

- List of law clerks of the Supreme Court of the United States

References

[1] See, eg, Katherine G Young, 'Open Chambers: High Court Associates and Supreme Court Clerks Compared' (2007) 31 *Melbourne University Law Review* 646, 657-61.

[2] http://www.scc-csc.gc.ca/empl/lc-aj/prog-eng.asp

[3] .http://www.ontariocourts.on.ca/coa/en/lawclerkprogram/index.htm

[4] .http://www.tribunaux.qc.ca/c-appel/English/Clerkship/clerkship.html

[5] James Kanter, "Obscure EU court may be ally for business", *International Herald Tribune*

[6] Décret n°96-513 du 7 juin 1996 relatif aux assistants de justice (In French (http://www.legifrance.gouv.fr/affichTexte.do?cidTexte=JORFTEXT000000193158&dateTexte=))

[7] District court for Paris, Seine-et-Marne, Val-de-Marne Essonne, Seine-Saint-Denis and Yonne departments.

[8] District Court for Yvelines, Hauts-de-Seine - which includes the business district of La Defense -, Val-d'Oise and Eure-et-Loir departments.

[9] Disctrict court for Alpes-de-Haute-Provence, Alpes-Maritimes, Bouches-du-Rhône and Var departments.

[10] District court for Morbihan, Finistère, Ille-et-Vilaine, Loire-Atlantique and Côtes-d'Armor departments.

[11] See article L227-1 Code de justice administrative (In French (http://www.legifrance.gouv.fr/affichTexte.do?cidTexte=JORFTEXT000000418872&dateTexte=)).

[12] Legally India report on judicial clerkships (http://www.legallyindia.com/201009231338/Law-schools/supreme-court-judicial-clerkship-stipends-hiked-to-rs-25k-attractive-enough)

[13] Courts Service Annual Report 2008 (www.courts.ie)

[14] http://www.domstol.se/templates/DV_InfoPage____2321.aspx

[15] http://www.domstol.se/templates/DV_InfoPage____2318.aspx

[16] Wayne L. Anderson and Marilyn J. Headrick, *The Legal Profession: Is it for you?* (Cincinnati: Thomson Executive Press, 1996), 110.

[17] "Appeals court judge a rising star among conservatives" (http://archives.cnn.com/2001/LAW/08/22/luttig.profile/). *CNN*. August 22, 2001. . Retrieved May 5, 2010.

[18] "Clerks Highlight Supreme Court's Polarization" (http://www.nytimes.com/2010/09/07/us/politics/07clerks.html) article by Adam Liptak in *The New York Times* September 6, 2010, accessed September 7, 2010

[19] "National Federal Judges Law Clerk Hiring Plan" Website, http://www.cadc.uscourts.gov/internet/lawclerk.nsf/Content/CriticalDates?OpenDocument

[20] Rudesill, Dakota S. (2008-11-05). "Keepers of the U.S. Code: The Case for a Congressional Clerkship Program" (http://lawreview.wustl.edu/slip-opinions/keepers-of-the-us-code-the-case-for-a-congressional-clerkship-program/). Slip Opinions, the online supplement to *Washington University Law Review*. . Retrieved 2009-02-22.

[21] James Chace, *Acheson: The Secretary of State Who Created the American World* (New York: Simon & Schuster, 2007 [1998]), 44.

[22] Itir Yakar, "Unseen Staff Attorneys Anchor State's Top Court: Institution's System of Permanent Employees Means Workers Can Outlast the Justices," *San Francisco Daily Journal*, 30 May 2006, 1.

Further reading

- Cohen, Jonathan Matthew (2002). *Inside Appellate Courts: The Impact of Court Organization on Judicial Decision Making in the United States Courts of Appeals*. Ann Arbor, MI: University of Michigan Press. ISBN 0472112562.
- Kenney, Sally J. (2000). "Beyond Principals and Agents: Seeing Courts as Organizations by Comparing Referendaires at the European Court of Justice and Law Clerks at the U.S. Supreme Court". *Comparative Political Studies* **33** (5): 593–625. doi:10.1177/0010414000033005002.
- Ward, Artemus; Weiden, David L. (2006). *Sorcerers' Apprentices: 100 Years of Law Clerks at the United States Supreme Court*. New York: NYU Press. ISBN 0814794041.

External links

- Federal Judicial Center page on Law Clerks (http://www.fjc.gov/history/home.nsf/page/admin_03_11.html)
- Searchable site for US federal law clerk vacancies (https://lawclerks.ao.uscourts.gov/)
- Openings for Law Clerks with the Los Angeles Superior Court (http://www.lasuperiorcourt.org/HR/)
- Description of available clerkships in Canada (http://www.law.uwo.ca/info-current/cso/2005Clerkship.htm)

United_States_Court_of_International_Trade

The **United States Court of International Trade** is an Article III court, with full powers in law and equity. The Customs Court Act of 1980 replaced the old United States Customs Court with the United States Court of International Trade. The Court has nine sitting Judges, as well as Senior Judges. The Court sits in New York City, although it is authorized to sit elsewhere, including in foreign nations.

The James L. Watson Court of International Trade Building on Foley Square

Jurisdiction

The Court possesses limited subject matter jurisdiction, meaning that it may hear only cases involving particular international trade and customs law questions. For example, the Court hears disputes such as those involving protests filed with U.S. Customs and Border Protection, decisions regarding Trade Adjustment Assistance by the United States Department of Labor or United States Department of Agriculture, customs broker licensing, and disputes relating to determinations made by the United States International Trade Commission and the Department of Commerce's International Trade Administration regarding antidumping and countervailing duties.

There is one notable exception to the Court's jurisdiction. In cases involving antidumping and countervailing duties imposed on Canadian or Mexican merchandise, an interested party can request that the case be heard before a special *ad hoc* binational panel organized under Chapter 19 of the 1988 Canadian-U.S. Free Trade Agreement.

Procedure

Most cases are heard by a single judge. If a case challenges the constitutionality of a U.S. law or has important implications regarding the administration or interpretation of the customs laws, then it may be heard by a three-judge panel. Many Judges of the Court of International Trade also regularly sit by designation on three-judge panels of the United States Court of Appeals for the Second Circuit.

Although the Court maintains its own rules of procedure, they are patterned for the most part on the Federal Rules of Civil Procedure. The court has held that decisions interpreting the Federal Rules of Civil Procedure are "instructive" in interpreting its own rules.

Appeals from the Court of International Trade are heard by the United States Court of Appeals for the Federal Circuit, which normally sits in Washington, D.C. Further appeals from the United States Court of Appeals for the Federal Circuit are heard by the Supreme Court of the United States.

Courthouse

The **James L. Watson Court of International Trade Building**, located on Foley Square in lower Manhattan in New York City, houses the court. It is also known as 1 Federal Plaza and is adjacent to the Jacob K. Javits Federal Building.

The building is named for James L. Watson, a judge of the United States Customs Court. The legislation naming the building for Watson was authored by U.S. Representative Charles Rangel of New York.[1]

Judges and Senior Judges (current as of June 2011)

There will be another vacancy on the court when Evan Wallach takes his commission to be a Circuit Judge for the United States Court of Appeals for the Federal Circuit, to which position he was confirmed by the Senate on November 8, 2011.

Judge	**Began active service**	**Ended active service**	**Ended senior service**	Appointed by
Jane A. Restani[2]	1983	-	-	Ronald Reagan
Gregory W. Carman[3]	1983	-	-	Ronald Reagan
Donald C. Pogue	1995	-	-	Bill Clinton
Evan Wallach	1995	-	-	Bill Clinton
Delissa A. Ridgway	1998	-	-	Bill Clinton
Richard K. Eaton	1999	-	-	Bill Clinton
Timothy C. Stanceu	2003	-	-	George W. Bush
Leo M. Gordon	2006	-	-	George W. Bush
(vacant since 2011-06-02 - formerly Barzilay)	*(n/a)*	*(n/a)*	*(n/a)*	*(n/a)*
Thomas J. Aquilino, Jr.	1985	2004	-	Ronald Reagan
Nicholas Tsoucalas	1986	1996	-	Ronald Reagan
R. Kenton Musgrave	1987	1997	-	Ronald Reagan
Richard W. Goldberg	1991	2001	-	George H.W. Bush
Judith M. Barzilay	1998	2011	-	Bill Clinton

Past Judges

Judge	Began active service	Ended active service	Ended senior service	Appointed by
James Lopez Watson	1966	1991	2001 (death)	Lyndon Johnson
Edward Dominic Re	1968	1991[4]	-	Lyndon Johnson
Bernard Newman	1968	1983	1999 (death)	Lyndon Johnson
Dominick L. DiCarlo	1984	1996[5]	2009 (death)	Ronald Reagan
Paul Peter Rao	1948	?	?	Harry Truman
Scovel Richardson	1957	?	?	Dwight Eisenhower
Frederick Landis, Jr.	1965	?	?	Lyndon Johnson
Herbert Naaman Maletz	1967	?	?	Lyndon Johnson
Samuel Murray Rosenstein	1968	?	?	Lyndon Johnson
Nils Andreas Boe	1971	?	?	Richard Nixon

U.S. Customs Court Judges

Judge	Began active service	Ended active service	Appointed by
Charles H. Ham	1890	1902	Benjamin Harrison
James A. Jewell	1890	1903	Benjamin Harrison
George H. Sharpe	1890	1900	Benjamin Harrison
Thaddeus S. Sharretts	1890	1913	Benjamin Harrison
Ferdinand N. Shurtleff	1890	1899	Benjamin Harrison
Henderson M. Somerville	1890	1915	Benjamin Harrison
Joseph Lewis Stackpole	1890	1891	Benjamin Harrison
George C. Tichenor	1890	1902	Benjamin Harrison
Joseph Biddle Wilkinson, Jr.	1890	1900	Benjamin Harrison
Wilbur Fisk Lunt	1891	1907	Benjamin Harrison
William Barberie Howell	1899	1927	William McKinley
Israel Fredrick Fischer	1899	1940	William McKinley
Marion De Vries	1900	1910	William McKinley
Byron Sylvester Waite	1902	1930	Theodore Roosevelt
Eugene Gano Hay	1903	1924	Theodore Roosevelt
Charles Paul McClelland	1903	1939	Theodore Roosevelt
Roy Chamberlain	1908	1913	Theodore Roosevelt
Samuel Bronson Cooper	1910	1918	William H. Taft
George Stewart Brown	1913	1941	Woodrow Wilson
Jerry Bartholomew Sullivan	1913	1948	Woodrow Wilson
William Charles Adamson	1917	1928	Woodrow Wilson

George Emery Weller	1919	1932	Woodrow Wilson
George M. Young	1924	1932	Calvin Coolidge
Genevieve Rose Cline	1928	1959	Calvin Coolidge
William Josiah Tilson	1928	1949	Calvin Coolidge
Walter Howard Evans	1931	1959	Herbert Hoover
David Hayes Kincheloe	1931	1950	Herbert Hoover
Fredrick William Dallinger	1932	1955	Herbert Hoover
William John Keefe	1933	1955	Franklin D. Roosevelt
Webster Oliver	1940	1969	Franklin D. Roosevelt
Thomas Joseph Walker	1940	1945	Franklin D. Roosevelt
William Purrington Cole	1942	1952	Franklin D. Roosevelt
William Alexander Ekwall	1942	1956	Franklin D. Roosevelt
Charles Drummond Lawrence	1943	1975	Franklin D. Roosevelt
Morgan Ford	1949	1980	Harry Truman
Jed Joseph Johnson	1947	1963	Harry Truman
Irving Charles Mollison	1945	1962	Harry Truman
Paul Peter Rao	1948	1980[6]	Harry Truman
David John Wilson	1954	1976	Dwight Eisenhower
Mary Donlon Alger	1955	1977	Dwight Eisenhower
Scovel Richardson	1957	1980[6]	Dwight Eisenhower
Philip Nichols, Jr.	1964	1966	Lyndon Johnson
Frederick Landis, Jr.	1965	1980[6]	Lyndon Johnson
James Lopez Watson	1966	1980[6]	Lyndon Johnson
Lindley Garrison Beckworth, Sr.	1967	1968	Lyndon Johnson
Herbert Naaman Maletz	1967	1980[6]	Lyndon Johnson
Bernard Newman	1968	1980[6]	Lyndon Johnson
Edward D. Re	1968	1980[6]	Lyndon Johnson
Samuel Murray Rosenstein	1968	1980[6]	Lyndon Johnson
Nils Andreas Boe	1971	1980[6]	Richard Nixon

References

[1] Press release (http://www.house.gov/list/press/ny15_rangel/CBRDedicatesWatsonCourtofInternationalTrade111003.html) from the office of Rep. Charles Rangel
[2] Current chief judge
[3] Past chief judge.
[4] appointed Chief Judge by Jimmy Carter in 1977
[5] chief judge from 1991 to 1996
[6] Reassigned to the Court of International Trade when the Customs Court was dissolved, receiving his commission on November 1, 1980.

External links

- United States Court of International Trade (http://www.cit.uscourts.gov), official site
- History of the court (http://www.fjc.gov/history/home.nsf/page/custom_cit_bdy) from the Federal Judicial Center

John_Wesley_Warrington

John Wesley Warrington		
[[file:John Wesley Warrington 1897.jpg		alt=]]
circa 1897		
United States Court of Appeals for the Sixth Circuit		
In office March 16, 1909 – October 6, 1919		
Appointed by	William Howard Taft	
Preceded by	John Kelvey Richards	
Succeeded by	Maurice H. Donahue	
Personal details		
Born	July 22, 1844Clark County, Ohio	
Died	May 26, 1921 (aged 76)Cincinnati, Ohio	
Alma mater	Cincinnati Law School	
Occupation	lawyer, professor	
Signature		
Military service		
Allegiance	United States of America	
Service/branch	Union Army	
Years of service	1862-1865	
Unit	110th Ohio Infantry	

John Wesley Warrington (July 22, 1844 - May 26, 1921) was a United States federal judge. John Wesley Warrington was, by family records, born on July 22, 1846, which made him but 16 years old when he enlisted in the 110th O.V.I.

Born in Clark County, Ohio, Warrington joined the United States Army during the American Civil War, serving in the 110th Ohio Infantry from 1862 to 1865. He thereafter attended the University of Cincinnati College of Law, receiving an LL.B. in 1869. He worked for the city of Cincinnati, Ohio, as an assistant city solicitor from 1869 to 1873, and then as city solicitor until 1875. He was a Republican Presidential elector for Hayes/Wheeler in 1876.[1] He was in private practice in Cincinnati from 1876 to 1909, during which time he was a professor of equity jurisprudence and trusts at the Cincinnati Law School, from 1901 to 1904.

On March 16, 1909, President William Howard Taft nominated Warrington to a seat on the United States Court of Appeals for the Sixth Circuit vacated by John Kelvey Richards. On the same day, Warrington was confirmed by the United States Senate, and received his commission. When Warrington assumed senior status on October 6, 1919, he was the first judge to enter this form of semi-retirement, which had recently been created by statute. He continued working in senior status until his death.

Sources

[1] Smith 1898 : 364

- John Wesley Warrington (http://www.fjc.gov/servlet/nGetInfo?jid=2509&cid=999&ctype=na&instate=na) at the *Biographical Directory of Federal Judges*, a public domain publication of the Federal Judicial Center.
- Smith, Joseph P, ed (1898). *History of the Republican Party in Ohio* (http://books.google.com/books?id=eaAFAAAAMAAJ&pg=PA364). I. Chicago: the Lewis Publishing Company.

Supreme_Court_of_Virginia

Virginia Supreme Court	
 The Supreme Court of Virginia building in Richmond.	
Established	1779
Jurisdiction	Virginia, United States
Location	Virginia
Authorized by	Virginia Constitution
Decisions are appealed to	Supreme Court of the United States

The **Supreme Court of Virginia** is the highest court in the Commonwealth of Virginia. It primarily hears appeals from the trial-level city and county Circuit Courts, as well as the criminal law, family law and administrative law cases that go through the Court of Appeals of Virginia. It is one of the oldest continuously active judicial bodies in the United States. It was known as the **Supreme Court of Appeals** until 1970, when it was renamed the Supreme Court of Virginia.

The present Supreme Court of Virginia is made up of seven justices elected by a majority vote of both houses of the General Assembly for a term of twelve years. To be eligible for election, a candidate must be a resident of Virginia and must have been a member of the Virginia Bar for at least five years. Vacancies on the court occurring between sessions of the General Assembly may be filled by the Governor for a term expiring thirty days after the commencement of the next session of the General Assembly. By statute, the Chief Justice is chosen by a majority vote of the seven justices.

By statute, the court may designate a retired justice to serve as Senior Justice for a renewable one year term. The court may designate up to five senior justices. Senior justices sit with the court during regular sessions hearing writs and sitting on merit cases, especially when an active member of the court is recused from hearing a particular case. In addition, a retired justice who has not been designated as a senior justice may sit with the court by special designation.

History of the Supreme Court of Virginia

The Supreme Court of Virginia has its roots in the seventeenth century English legal system, which was instituted in Virginia as part of the Charter of 1606 under which Jamestown, Virginia, the first permanent English settlement in North America, was established. In 1623, the Virginia House of Burgesses created a five-man appellate court, which met quarterly to hear appeals from the lower courts. Meeting on the first day of March, June, September, and December, it became known as the Quarter Court.

The June term became unnecessary over the years, and in 1661, the Quarter Court became the General Court with original and appellate jurisdiction in both civil and criminal matters. It was a court of last resort for the Virginia colonists except in those rare circumstances when an appeal could be made to the King in England. Its members were appointed by the King on the basis of social standing, property, and the proximity of their estates to the

Williamsburg capital. Though the judges were generally most capable, the majority possessed no formal legal training.

At the close of the Revolutionary War, the court system was reorganized. An act of the new General Assembly in 1779 created four superior courts, including the Supreme Court of Appeals, to be composed of judges of the other three existing courts: the Admiralty, the General, and the Chancery Courts. The Supreme Court of Appeals, which served as a model for the United States Supreme Court, first convened in Williamsburg on August 30, 1779. Shortly thereafter, the Court was moved to Richmond and held its sessions in the Henrico County Courthouse. Its jurisdiction was primarily appellate, and its members were elected by the legislature.

Among the court's first members were several distinguished legal scholars and jurists as well as leaders of the revolutionary period. Edmund Pendleton, who served Virginia as a delegate to the First Continental Congress, was selected by the judges as its first president. George Wythe, the mentor of Thomas Jefferson and signer of the Declaration of Independence, and John Blair, who later served on the United States Supreme Court, were also members of Virginia's first Supreme Court. Another notable member was William Fleming, who also served as the third governor of Virginia.

Until 1788, the judges did not render written opinions or give reasons for their decisions. Pendleton felt that the policy of no written opinions preserved a semblance of unity for the court and lent more credence to their decisions. Thomas Jefferson disagreed and began recording the decisions of the court in his reports. The court convened on the tenth day of April and met for twenty-four days unless they were able to complete their business sooner.

A legislative act of 1788 provided that the court should be entirely separated from the other courts with five judges to be elected by joint vote of both houses of the General Assembly. These men were commissioned by the Governor and appointed for life on good behavior. This resulted in placing the judges beyond control of the legislature once on the bench, and the court continued to function in this manner for more than half a century.

The Reform Convention of 1850-51 again reorganized the judiciary by limiting the terms of the justices to twelve years and providing for their election by popular vote. The state was divided into five judicial sections, and each candidate was required to be at least thirty-five years old and to reside within the section he wished to represent. The resulting Constitution of 1851 also required the court to state in writing its reasons for reversing or affirming a judgment or a decree.

Following the turmoil of the Civil War, the Constitution of 1870 altered the method of selecting judges and reestablished election by joint vote of both houses of the General Assembly, retaining the term of twelve years. The constitution also required that annual sessions be held away from Richmond in the localities of Wytheville, Staunton, and Winchester. This mandate from the days of horse and buggy travel continued into the twentieth century, with sessions being held in Staunton as late as September, 1970. In recent years, however, the court has held writ panel sessions outside of Richmond during the summer. These sessions are held for the convenience of the attorneys who would otherwise have to travel to Richmond and also to provide a higher profile for the court outside of Richmond.

By constitutional amendment in 1928, the number of justices was increased to seven and the title of the presiding officer of the court was changed from President to Chief Justice. At the same time, the amendment significantly increased the power given the Supreme Court.

The Constitution of 1970 changed the name of the court to its present title of *Supreme Court of Virginia.*

Judicial Performance Evaluation Program controversy

The Virginia General Assembly directed the Court by statute to create a judicial performance evaluation (JPE) program in order to have some objective measure for determining whether to reappoint judges at the end of their terms. In 2008, the reports on the first five judges to be evaluated in the program were sent to the chairmen of the Senate and House Courts of Justice committees; however, the Court also entered an order directing the chairmen to disseminate the reports only to the members of the legislature and to collect all copies at the end of the session and return them to the Court. The order expressly stated that the reports were confidential and could not be released to the public.

Rather than abide by the terms of this order, the chairman refused to accept the reports, and the committees declined to interview the five judges who were the subject of the report. Several legislators viewed the Court's order as a violation of separation of powers. This controversy also led to the introduction of legislation that would take the evaluation program away from the Court's control and, instead, make it subject to direct control by the General Assembly. Another bill was also introduced to limit the terms of the Chief Justice of the Court to two consecutive four-year terms. Not coincidentally, Chief Justice Hassell, who was at the center of the controversy, was then serving his second term as head of the Court.

Neither of these bills passed, however the legislature did eliminate the specific line-item funding for the JPE program. Because the statute directing the Court to maintain the program remains in force, a number of members of the legislature indicated that they expected the Court to continue the program by finding funds from elsewhere in the Judicial Branch's budget. However, as the Court was already being required to make cuts in its budget due to the economic downturn, the Court advised the judges currently under evaluation that the program would be suspended at the end of the current fiscal year on June 30, 2009.

Jurisdiction of the Virginia Supreme Court

Although the Supreme Court of Virginia possesses both original and appellate jurisdiction, its primary function is to review decisions of lower courts, including the Court of Appeals, from which appeals have been allowed. Virginia does not allow an appeal to the Supreme Court as a matter of right except in cases involving the State Corporation Commission, the disbarment of an attorney, and review of the death penalty.

The court's original jurisdiction is limited to cases of habeas corpus (ordering one holding custody to produce the detained person before the court for the purpose of determining whether such custody is proper), mandamus (ordering the holder of an office to perform his duty), prohibition (ordering an action stopped in a lower court), and writs of actual innocence pursuant to Virginia's Code § 19.2-327.2. It also has original jurisdiction for challenges to decisions of the State Corporation Commission pursuant to Article IX of the Constitution of Virginia[1]. The Supreme Court also has original jurisdiction in matters filed by the Judicial Inquiry and Review Commission relating to judicial censure, retirement, and removal of judges.

Procedure

The court meets for five-day sessions beginning in September and continuing every seventh week thereafter until the completion of the June docket. All sessions are held in Richmond. During the six-week recess between each session, the justices conduct extensive legal research upon the cases awaiting decision, draft and review opinions, study cases in which petitions for appeal have been filed, conduct hearings on petitions for appeal, and attend to administrative duties.

In Virginia, appellate review before the Supreme Court is a two step process in most cases. First, a petition is filed with the Clerk of the Supreme Court. Petitions are then assigned to a law clerk or staff attorney for research and further preparation. Oral arguments are heard before a panel of three justices. In a limited number of cases, oral arguments may be heard by the Chief Staff Attorney who then presents the case to a panel of three justices for decision. The justices conduct a thorough review on the merits of each case with the assistance of memoranda summarizing the facts and basic issues of each appeal prepared by a law clerk or staff attorney. One justice may grant an appeal, even if the other two justices do not concur. Usually, three justices must concur before an appeal is denied (in rare cases, two justices may consider a case for which there has been no oral argument to the Court or which is being dismissed for procedural reasons). If the petition is denied, the appeal process ends (except that the appellant may request a rehearing) and the judgment of the lower court is affirmed. If the petition is granted, the second phase of the appeal proceeds with eventual argument of the cases before the full court.

During the second phase of an appeal and before each session of the court, the Clerk forwards to each justice a copy of the printed docket showing the cases to be heard at that session, together with a copy of the printed record and briefs filed in each case. This allows each justice to study the cases before they are argued orally.

A rotation system is used in designating the justices who are to prepare the opinions of the court. Prior to each session of the court, the assignment of the cases is determined by lot. Seven slips of paper are prepared by the Clerk of the Court with one slip bearing the number "I" and the remainder being blank. The slips are placed in a hat, and the member of the court (or a proxy) drawing the marked paper writes opinions in the first, eighth, and fifteenth, etc., cases on the docket. The justice immediately below him/her in seniority is responsible for the second, ninth, and sixteenth cases, and so on until all cases are assigned.

Sessions are held in the Courtroom of the Supreme Court with the justices being seated on the bench in order of seniority. The Chief Justice is seated in the center with the justice next in seniority on his right, the justice third in seniority on his left, and so on in alternating order such that the newest justice is seated on the far left. Attorneys for both sides are usually allowed fifteen minutes each to present their arguments. The justices often interrupt the attorneys to ask questions on some issue in the case. During a typical session of the court, the justices hear oral arguments each morning and convene that afternoon for a private discussion of the cases heard that morning. The member responsible for writing the opinion directs discussion of the case by asking the justice seated at the conference table to the right for comments on the case. The justices then proceed to comment in turn with the member designated to write the opinion speaking last. This discussion and debate provide the opinion writer guidance in preparing an opinion reflecting the views of a majority of the justices. Once a justice has completed a draft of his opinion, copies are circulated to the other members of the court and the Court Reporter. Opinion conferences are held prior to the beginning of each session. At this time, the justices conclude their review of the cases and the draft opinions receive final approval. Opinions are made public on the last day of each session of the court and are published in the *Virginia Reports*.

Court organization

The court organization consists of the Clerk of the Supreme Court, the Executive Secretary of the Supreme Court, the Court Reporter, the Chief Staff Attorney of the Supreme Court, and the Law Librarian.

The Clerk is appointed by and serves at the pleasure of the Supreme Court. The Clerk's Office receives, processes, and maintains permanent records of all appeals and other official documents filed with the Court. The Clerk also maintains records of qualified attorneys and other administrative records. The current Clerk is Patricia Harrington. Her Chief Deputy is Doug Robelen.

The Executive Secretary is appointed by and serves at the pleasure of the Supreme Court. At one time, it was required that the Executive Secretary be a resident of the Commonwealth and a member of the Virginia Bar for at least five years. However, upon the retirement of the Robert Baldwin, the long severing Executive Secretary, in 2004, and after an extensive search for a replacement failed to find a suitable candidate who was an attorney, the latter requirement was waived so that Karl R. Hade, an employee of the Executive Secretary's Office of Judicial Information and Technology could assume the role. Hade is expected to usher in a new era of technology-enhanced court services. A new position of Counsel to the Executive Secretary was created to advise the Executive Secretary on legal matters. The purpose of the office is to provide assistance to the Chief Justice and the court in the administration of the judicial system.

The Chief Staff Attorney is appointed by and serves at the pleasure of the Supreme Court. He supervises a staff of permanent staff attorneys, law clerks and paralegals. The current Chief Staff Attorney is Gregory Lucyk, a former Virginia Assistant Attorney General.

Each justice has two personal law clerks who, along with other assigned duties, assists with legal research and perfection of opinions. The law clerks and staff attorneys are also principally responsible for reviewing the petitions for appeal which are filed as a prerequisite to the court granting an appeal.

The Court Reporter is a distinguished member of the faculty of one of the law schools in Virginia. His main responsibility is to supervise the compilation, indexing, printing and publication of the written opinions of the court in the *Virginia Reports*. He is assisted by a fulltime staff attorney. There are over two hundred and seventy volumes of the Reports which, together with the Constitution of Virginia and the Acts of the General Assembly of Virginia (but subject to federal law) form the body of law by which all Virginians are governed. The current Court Reporter is Prof. Kent Sinclair of the University of Virginia School of Law.

The State Law Librarian supervises a library of approximately 100,000 volumes for the use of the court and the Bar. The current State Law Librarian is Gail Warren. The State Law Library also serves as an official Federal Depository Library, meaning that it receives official publications of the United States Government, such as the Congressional Record, so that the public may have access to these documents.

The Virginia judicial system

Article VI, Section 4, of the Constitution of Virginia places upon the Chief Justice of the Supreme Court of Virginia the responsibility of supervising the administration of the entire court system of the Commonwealth. The Chief Justice may temporarily assign any judge of a circuit court to any other circuit court and may recall a retired circuit court judge to active duty. The Chief Justice may also designate a retired judge, an active district court judge, or an active circuit court judge, with his/her consent, to assist with a congested workload in any district. Other responsibilities of the Chief Justice include presiding over the various committees charged with improving the administration of justice in Virginia.

The Virginia judicial system comprises the Supreme Court, a Court of Appeals, circuit courts in thirty-one judicial circuits, general district and juvenile and domestic relations district courts in thirty-two districts, and magistrates in offices in thirty-two districts. Three advisory/administrative bodies have been created by the legislature to aid in the operation of the court system: the Judicial Inquiry and Review Commission, the Judicial Council, and the Committee on District Courts.

The aim of the Virginia judicial system is to assure that disputes are resolved justly, promptly, and economically through a court system unified in its structures and administration. A competent staff of judges and court personnel, uniform rules and practices, and adequate funding are necessary to accomplish this function and to provide the citizens of the Commonwealth of Virginia with the best possible judicial system.

Court seal

Though it is seldom used except on the admissions certificates issued to members of the Virginia State Bar, the Supreme Court has its own seal which is distinct from the Seal of Virginia. The Court's seal depicts the Goddess Justitia seated on a throne holding the Scales of Justice in her left hand while her right hand extends toward the figure of an ostrich (some descriptions identify the bird as an ibis, crane or egret), a symbol of mercy or rumination of thought. The origin of the seal is not known. During a ceremony to celebrate the Court's 225th anniversary, the seal was used for the first time in many years on the cover of the programs given to guests, and also appears on certificates of admission and other ceremonial documents issued by the Court. The lesser state seal, however, is depicted on the Justices' chairs and on a medallion over the entrance to the main courtroom.

Current Composition of the Court

Active

Judge	Born	First elected	Expiration [2]	Chief	Note
Cynthia D. Kinser	1951	1998	January 31, 2022	2011-2015	[3]
Donald W. Lemons	1948	2000	March 16, 2012	—	
S. Bernard Goodwyn	1961	2008	February 8, 2020	—	
Leroy F. Millette, Jr.		2009	January 31, 2021	—	[4]
William C. Mims	1957	2010	March 31, 2022	—	
Elizabeth A. McClanahan	September 1, 1959	2011	July 31, 2023	—	
Cleo E. Powell		2011	July 31, 2023	—	

Senior

Judge	Born	Active service	Chief	Senior since
Harry L. Carrico	1916	1961-2003	1981-2003	2003
Charles S. Russell	1926	1982-1991	—	2004
Elizabeth B. Lacy	1945	1988-2007	—	2007
Lawrence L. Koontz, Jr.	1940	1995-2011	—	2011

Living Former Members

- Hon. Henry H. Whiting, Retired Justice
- Hon. G. Steven Agee, former Justice (Justice Agee resigned from the Court in order to take his seat on the federal Fourth Circuit Court of Appeals; so long as he remains on active service in the federal court system, he will be ineligible for recall to service on the Court)
- Hon. John Charles Thomas, former Justice (because Justice Thomas returned to the practice of law after he resigned from the court, he is not currently subject to recall for service on the Court)
- Hon. Barbara Milano Keenan, former Justice (Justice Keenan resigned from the Court in order to take her seat on the federal Fourth Circuit Court of Appeals; so long as she remains on active service in the federal court system, she will be ineligible for recall to service on the Court)

References

[1] http://legis.state.va.us/Laws/search/Constitution.htm#9S1

[2] "Justices of the Supreme Court of Virginia" (http://www.courts.state.va.us/courts/scv/supreme.html). Office of the Executive Secretary, Supreme Court of Virginia. . Retrieved 30 June 2011.

[3] Justice Kinser will reach the mandatory retirement age for Virginia jurists upon expiration of her term as a Justice; she will have to retire or take senior status no later than January 2022.

[4] Justice Millette will reach the mandatory retirement age for Virginia jurists before the expiration of his term; under current law, he will have to retire or take senior status no later than January 2020.

- The Supreme Court of Virginia (http://www.courts.state.va.us/scv/home.html).
- Supreme Court of Virginia is at coordinates 37°32′23″N 77°26′08″W

Iowa_Court_of_Appeals

The **Iowa Court of Appeals** is the intermediate-level appellate court of the state of Iowa. Its purpose is to review appeals from trial court decisions which are referred to the court by the Iowa Supreme Court. The court decides the vast majority of appeals filed from trial courts in the state of Iowa, and its decisions are final unless further review is granted by the Iowa Supreme Court.

Judges of the court

The court is composed of nine judges. Each judge is appointed for one year by the governor, from a list of nominees composed by the State Judicial Nominating Commission. The judge will then serve a one-year term before facing a retention election. If the judge is reelected, his/her term will normally be six years. Retirement age is 72, after which some judges go on senior status.

The judges elect the Chief Judge from amongst themselves every two years. The chief judge functions as the administrative head of the court.

As of 2010, the nine judges are:

- Chief Judge Rosemary Shaw Sackett
- Gayle Nelson Vogel
- Anuradha Vaitheswaran
- Larry J. Eisenhauer
- Amanda Potterfield
- Richard H. Doyle
- Edward Mansfield
- David Danilson
- Mary Tabor

See also

- Courts of Iowa

External links

- Homepage of the Iowa Court of Appeals [1]
- Judges of the Iowa Court of Appeals [2]

References

[1] http://www.iowacourts.gov/Court_of_Appeals/
[2] http://www.iowacourts.gov/Court_of_Appeals/Judges/

Virginia

Commonwealth of Virginia

Flag

Seal

Nickname(s): *Old Dominion; Mother of Presidents*

Motto(s): *Sic Semper Tyrannis (Latin)*[1]

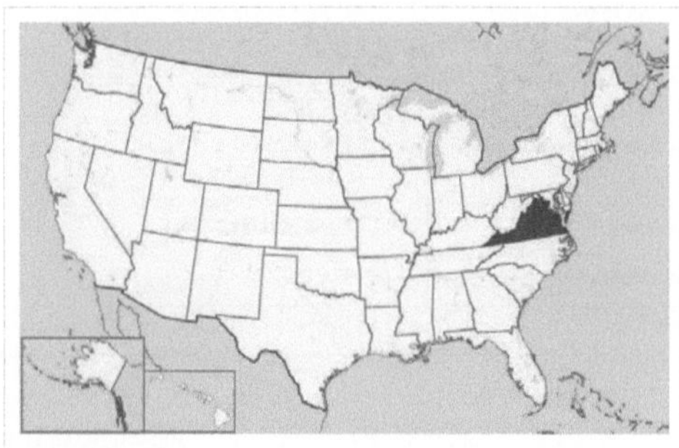

Official language(s)	English
Spoken language(s)	English 94.6%, Spanish 5.9%
Demonym	Virginian
Capital	Richmond
Largest city	Virginia Beach
Largest metro area	Northern Virginia
Area	Ranked 35th in the U.S.
- Total	42,774.2 sq mi (110,785.67 km^2)
- Width	200 miles (320 km)
- Length	430 miles (690 km)
- % water	7.4
- Latitude	36° 32′ N to 39° 28′ N
- Longitude	75° 15′ W to 83° 41′ W
Population	Ranked 12th in the U.S.
- Total	8,001,024[2]
- Density	202.6/sq mi (78/km^2) Ranked 16th in the U.S.
- Median income	$61,044[3] (8th)

Elevation	
- Highest point	Mount Rogers[4] [5] 5,729 ft (1746 m)
- Mean	950 ft (290 m)
- Lowest point	Atlantic Ocean[4] sea level
Admission to Union	June 25, 1788 (10th)
Governor	Bob McDonnell (R)
Lieutenant Governor	Bill Bolling (R)
Legislature	General Assembly
- Upper house	Senate
- Lower house	House of Delegates
U.S. Senators	Jim Webb (D) Mark Warner (D)
U.S. House delegation	8 Republicans, 3 Democrats (list)
Time zone	Eastern: UTC−5/−4
Abbreviations	VA US-VA
Website	[www.virginia.gov www.virginia.gov]

Virginia (i/vər'dʒɪnjə/) is a U.S. state on the Atlantic Coast of the Southern United States. Virginia is nicknamed the "Old Dominion" and sometimes the "Mother of Presidents" after the eight U.S. presidents born there. The geography and climate of the Commonwealth are shaped by the Blue Ridge Mountains and the Chesapeake Bay, which provide habitat for much of its flora and fauna. The capital of the Commonwealth is Richmond; Virginia Beach is the most populous city and Fairfax County the most populous political subdivision. The Commonwealth's population is over eight million.[2]

The area's history begins with several indigenous groups, including the Powhatan. In 1607 the London Company established the Colony of Virginia as the first permanent New World English colony. Slave labor and the land acquired from displaced Native American tribes each played a significant role in the colony's early politics and plantation economy. Virginia was one of the 13 Colonies in the American Revolution and joined the Confederacy in the American Civil War, during which Richmond was made the Confederate capital and Virginia's northwestern counties separated to form the state of West Virginia. Although the Commonwealth was under conservative single party rule for nearly a century following Reconstruction, both major national parties are competitive in modern Virginia.[6]

The Virginia General Assembly is the oldest legislature in the Americas. The state government has been repeatedly ranked most effective by the Pew Center on the States.[7] It is unique in how it treats cities and counties equally, manages local roads, and prohibits its governors from serving consecutive terms. Virginia's economy has many sectors: agriculture in the Shenandoah Valley; federal agencies in Northern Virginia, including the headquarters of the Department of Defense and CIA; and military facilities in Hampton Roads, the site of the region's main seaport. Virginia's public schools and many colleges and universities have contributed to growing media and technology sectors. As a result, computer chips have become the state's leading export.[8]

Geography

Virginia has a total area of 42774.2 square miles (km^2), including 3180.13 square miles (8236.5 km^2) of water, making it the 35th-largest state by area.[9] Virginia is bordered by Maryland and Washington, D.C. to the north and east; by the Atlantic Ocean to the east; by North Carolina and Tennessee to the south; by Kentucky to the west; and by West Virginia to the north and west. Virginia's boundary with Maryland and Washington, D.C. extends to the low-water mark of the south shore of the Potomac River.[10] The southern border is defined as the 36° 30′ parallel north, though surveyor error led to deviations of as much as three arcminutes.[11]

Geology and terrain

The Chesapeake Bay separates the contiguous portion of the Commonwealth from the two-county peninsula of Virginia's Eastern Shore. The bay was formed following a meteoroid impact crater during the Eocene.[12] Many of Virginia's rivers flow into the Chesapeake Bay, including the Potomac, Rappahannock, York, and James, which create three peninsulas in the bay.[13] [14] Geographically and geologically, Virginia is divided into five regions from east to west: Tidewater, Piedmont, Blue Ridge Mountains, Ridge and Valley, and Cumberland Plateau.[15]

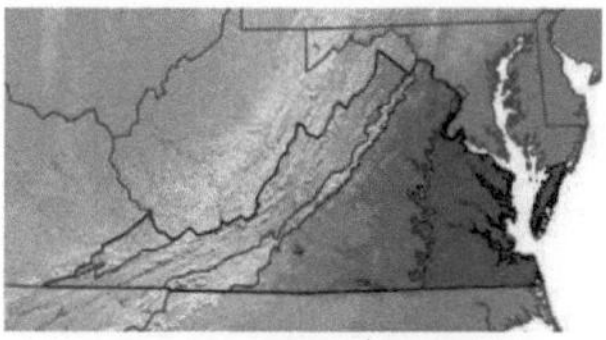

Virginia is divided into five geographic regions.

The Tidewater is a coastal plain between the Atlantic coast and the fall line. It includes the Eastern Shore and major estuaries of Chesapeake Bay. The Piedmont is a series of sedimentary and igneous rock-based foothills east of the mountains which were formed in the Mesozoic.[16] The region, known for its heavy clay soil, includes the Southwest Mountains.[17] The Blue Ridge Mountains are a physiographic province of the chain of Appalachian Mountains with the highest points in the state, the tallest being Mount Rogers at 5729 feet (1746 m).[18] The Ridge and Valley region is west of the mountains, and includes the Great Appalachian Valley. The region is carbonate rock based, and includes Massanutten Mountain.[19] The Cumberland Plateau and the Cumberland Mountains are in the south-west corner of Virginia, below the Allegheny Plateau. In this region rivers flow northwest, with a dendritic drainage system, into the Ohio River basin.[20]

Deciduous and evergreen trees give the Blue Ridge Mountains their distinct color[21]

The state's carbonate rock is filled with more than 4,000 caves, ten of which are open for tourism.[22] The Virginia seismic zone has not had a history of regular activity. Earthquakes are rarely above 4.5 on the Richter magnitude scale because Virginia is located away from the edges of the North American Plate. The largest earthquake, at an estimated 5.9 magnitude, was in 1897 near Blacksburg.[23] A 5.8 magnitude earthquake struck central Virginia on August 23, 2011, near Mineral. The earthquake was reportedly felt as far away as Toronto, Canada.[24] Coal mining takes place in the three mountainous regions at 40 distinct coal beds near Mesozoic basins.[25] Other resources such as slate, kyanite, sand, and gravel are mined, with an annual value of nearly $2 billion as of 2006.[26]

Climate

The climate of Virginia becomes increasingly warmer and more humid farther south and east.[27] Seasonal extremes vary from average lows of 26 °F (–3 °C) in January to average highs of 86 °F (30 °C) in July. The Atlantic ocean has a strong effect on eastern and southeastern coastal areas of the state. Influenced by the Gulf Stream, coastal weather is subject to hurricanes, most pronouncedly near the mouth of Chesapeake Bay.[28]

Virginia has an annual average of 35–45 days of thunderstorm activity, particularly in the western part of the state,[29] and an average annual precipitation of 42.7 inches (1085 mm).[28] Cold air masses arriving over the mountains in winter can lead to significant snowfalls, such as the Blizzard of 1996 and winter storms of 2009–2010. The interaction of these elements with the state's topography creates distinct microclimates in the Shenandoah Valley, the mountainous southwest, and the coastal plains.[30] Virginia averages seven tornadoes annually, most F2 or lower on the Fujita scale.[31]

In recent years, the expansion of the southern suburbs of Washington, D.C. into Northern Virginia has introduced an urban heat island primarily caused by increased absorption of solar radiation in more densely populated areas.[32] In the American Lung Association's 2011 report, 11 counties received failing grades for air quality, with Fairfax County having the worst in the state, due to automobile pollution.[33] [34] Haze in the mountains is caused in part by coal power plants.[35]

Flora and fauna

Forests cover 65% of the state, primarily with deciduous, broad leaf trees.[36] Lower altitudes are more likely to have small but dense stands of moisture-loving hemlocks and mosses in abundance, with hickory and oak in the Blue Ridge.[27] However since the early 1990s, Gypsy moth infestations have eroded the dominance of oak forests.[37] In the lowland tidewater yellow pines tend to dominate, with bald cypress wetland forests in the Great Dismal and Nottoway swamps. Other common trees and plants include chestnut, maple, tulip poplar, mountain laurel, milkweed, daisies, and many species of ferns. The largest areas of wilderness are along the Atlantic coast and in the western mountains, where the largest populations of trillium wildflowers in North America are found.[27] [38] The Atlantic coast regions are host to flora commonly associated with the South Atlantic pine forests and lower Southeast Coastal Plain maritime flora, the latter found primarily in southeastern Virginia.

White-tailed deer, also known as Virginia deer, graze at Tanner Ridge in Shenandoah National Park

Mammals include White-tailed deer, black bear, beaver, bobcat, coyote, raccoon, skunk, groundhog, Virginia Opossum, gray fox, and eastern cottontail rabbit.[39] Birds include cardinals, barred owls, Carolina chickadees, Red-tailed Hawks, Ospreys, Bald Eagles, and Wild Turkeys. The Peregrine Falcon was reintroduced into Shenandoah National Park in the mid-1990s.[40] Walleye, brook trout, Roanoke bass, and blue catfish are among the 210 known species of freshwater fish.[41] Running brooks with rocky bottoms are often inhabited by a plentiful amounts of crayfish and salamanders.[27] The Chesapeake Bay is host to many species, including blue crabs, clams, oysters, and rockfish (also known as striped bass).[42]

Virginia has 30 National Park Service units, such as Great Falls Park and the Appalachian Trail, and one national park, the Shenandoah National Park.[43] Shenandoah was established in 1935 and encompasses the scenic Skyline Drive. Almost 40% of the park's area (79,579 acres/322 km^2) has been designated as wilderness under the National Wilderness Preservation System.[44] Additionally, there are 34 Virginia state parks and 17 state forests, run by the Department of Conservation and Recreation and the Department of Forestry.[36] [45] The Chesapeake Bay, while not a national park, is protected by both state and federal legislation, and the jointly run Chesapeake Bay Program which conducts restoration on the bay and its watershed. The Great Dismal Swamp National Wildlife Refuge extends into North Carolina.[46] The Back Bay National Wildlife Refuge marks the beginning of the Outer Banks which also extends into North Carolina.

History

Jamestown 2007 marked Virginia's quadricentennial year, celebrating 400 years since the establishment of the Jamestown Colony. The celebrations highlighted contributions from Native Americans, Europeans, and Africans, each which had a significant part in shaping Virginia's history.[47] [48] Warfare, including among these groups, has also had an important role. Virginia was a focal point in conflicts from the French and Indian War, the American Revolution and the Civil War, to the Cold War and the War on Terrorism.[49] Stories about historic figures, such as those surrounding Pocahontas and John Smith, George Washington's childhood, or the plantation elite in the slave society of the antebellum period, have also created potent myths of state history, and have served as rationales for Virginia's ideology.[50]

A 19th-century depiction of Pocahontas, of the Powhatan tribe, an ancestor of many of the First Families of Virginia

Colony

The first people are estimated to have arrived in Virginia over 12,000 years ago.[51] By 5,000 years ago more permanent settlements emerged, and farming began by 900 AD. By 1500, the Algonquian peoples had founded towns such as Werowocomoco in the Tidewater region, which they referred to as *Tsenacommacah*. The other major language groups in the area were the Siouan to the west, and the Iroquoians, who included the Nottoway and Meherrin, to the north and south. After 1570, the Algonquians consolidated under Chief Powhatan in response to threats from these other groups on their trade network.[52] Powhatan controlled more than 30 smaller tribes and over 150 settlements, who shared a common Virginia Algonquian language. In 1607, the native Tidewater population was between 13,000 to 14,000.[53]

In 1583, Queen Elizabeth I of England granted Walter Raleigh a charter to explore and plant a colony north of Spanish Florida.[54] In 1584, Raleigh sent an expedition to the Atlantic coast of North America.[55] The name "Virginia" may have been suggested then by Raleigh or Elizabeth, perhaps noting her status as the "Virgin Queen", and may also be related to a native phrase, "Wingandacoa", or name, "Wingina".[56] Initially the name applied to the entire coastal region from South Carolina to Maine, plus the island of Bermuda.[57] The London Company was incorporated as a joint stock company by the proprietary Charter of 1606, which granted land rights to this area. The Company financed the first permanent English settlement in the "New World", Jamestown. Named for King James I, it was founded in May 1607 by Christopher Newport.[58] In 1619, colonists took greater control with an elected legislature called the House of Burgesses. With the bankruptcy of the London Company in 1624, the settlement was taken into royal authority as a British crown colony.[59]

Williamsburg was the capital from 1699 to 1780.

Life in the colony was perilous, and many died during the "starving time" in 1609 and the Anglo-Powhatan Wars, including the Indian massacre of 1622, which fostered the colonists' negative view of all tribes.[60] [61] By 1624, only 3,400 of the 6,000 early settlers had survived.[62] However, European demand for tobacco fueled the arrival of more settlers and servants.[63] The headright system tried to solve the labor shortage by providing colonists with land for each indentured servant they transported to Virginia.[64] African workers were first imported in 1619, and their slavery was codified after a 1654 lawsuit over the servant John Casor.[65]

Tensions and the geographic differences between the working and ruling classes led to Bacon's Rebellion in 1676, by which time current and former indentured servants made up as much as 80% of the population.[66] Rebels, largely from the colony's frontier, were also opposed to the conciliatory policy towards native tribes. Colonists appropriated tribal land by force and treaty, including the Treaty of 1677, which made the signatory tribes tributary states.

Williamsburg became the colonial capital in 1699, following the founding of The College of William & Mary in 1693.[67] In 1747, a group of Virginian speculators formed the Ohio Company, with the backing of the British crown, to start English settlement and trade in the Ohio Country west of the Appalachian Mountains.[68] France, which claimed this area as part of their colony of New France, viewed this as a threat, and the ensuing French and Indian War became part of the Seven Years War (1756–1763). A militia from several British colonies, called the Virginia Regiment, was led by then-Lieutenant colonel George Washington.[69]

Statehood

The British Parliament's efforts to levy new taxes following the French and Indian War were deeply unpopular in the colonies. In the House of Burgesses, opposition to taxation without representation was led by Patrick Henry and Richard Henry Lee, among others.[70] Virginians began to coordinate their actions with other colonies in 1773, and sent delegates to the Continental Congress the following year.[71] After the House of Burgesses was dissolved by the royal governor in 1774, Virginia's revolutionary leaders continued to govern via the Virginia Conventions. On May 15, 1776, the Convention declared Virginia's independence from the British Empire and adopted George Mason's Virginia Declaration of Rights, which was then included in a new constitution.[72] Another Virginian, Thomas Jefferson, drew upon Mason's work in drafting the national Declaration of Independence.[73]

1851 painting of Patrick Henry's speech before the House of Burgesses on the Virginia Resolves against the Stamp Act of 1765

When the American Revolutionary War began, George Washington was selected to head the colonial army. During the war, the capital was moved to Richmond at the urging of Governor Thomas Jefferson, who feared that Williamsburg's location would make it vulnerable to British attack.[74] In 1781, the combined action of Continental and French land and naval forces trapped the British army on the Virginia Peninsula, where troops under George Washington and Comte de Rochambeau defeated British General Cornwallis in the Siege of Yorktown. His surrender on October 19, 1781, led to peace negotiations in Paris and secured the independence of the colonies.[75]

Virginians were instrumental in writing the United States Constitution. James Madison drafted the Virginia Plan in 1787 and the Bill of Rights in 1789.[73] Virginia ratified the Constitution on June 25, 1788. The three-fifths compromise ensured that Virginia, with its large number of slaves, initially had the largest bloc in the House of Representatives. Together with the Virginia dynasty of presidents, this gave the Commonwealth national importance. In 1790, both Virginia and Maryland ceded territory to form the new District of Columbia, though the Virginian area was retroceded in 1846.[76] Virginia is sometimes called "Mother of States" because of its role in being carved into states like Kentucky, which became the 15th state in 1792, and for the numbers of American pioneers born in Virginia.[77]

Civil War and aftermath

Richmond, the capital of the Confederate States of America, was burned prior to its capture by the Union.

In addition to agriculture, slave labor was increasingly used in mining, shipbuilding and other industries.[78] Nat Turner's slave rebellion in 1831 and John Brown's Raid on Harpers Ferry in 1859 showed deep social discontent about slavery and its role in the plantation economy. By 1860, almost half a million people, roughly 31% of the total population of Virginia, were enslaved.[79] This division contributed to the start of the American Civil War.

Virginia voted to secede from the United States on April 17, 1861, after the Battle of Fort Sumter and Abraham Lincoln's call for volunteers. On April 24, Virginia joined the Confederate States of America, which chose Richmond as its capital.[77] After the 1863 Wheeling Convention, 48 counties in the northwest separated to form a new state of West Virginia, which chose to remain loyal to the Union. During the war, more battles were fought in Virginia than anywhere else, including Bull Run, the Seven Days Battles, Chancellorsville, and the concluding Battle of Appomattox Court House.[80] After the capture of Richmond in 1865, the capital was briefly moved to Danville.[81] Virginia was formally restored to the United States in 1870, due to the work of the Committee of Nine.[82]

During the post-war Reconstruction era, Virginia adopted a constitution which provided for free public schools, and guaranteed political, civil, and voting rights.[83] The populist Readjuster Party ran an inclusive coalition until the conservative white Democratic Party gained power after 1883.[84] It passed segregationist Jim Crow laws and in 1902 rewrote the Constitution of Virginia to include a poll tax and other voter registration measures that effectively disfranchised most African Americans and many poor whites until federal legislation was passed in the 1960s.[85] Though their schools were segregated and underfunded, as were services, due to a lack of political representation, African Americans were able to create their own communities.[86]

Contemporary era

The Virginia Civil Rights Memorial was erected in 2008 to commemorate the protests which led to school desegregation.

Protests started by Barbara Rose Johns in 1951 in Farmville against segregated schools led to the lawsuit *Davis v. County School Board of Prince Edward County*. This case, filed by Richmond natives Spottswood Robinson and Oliver Hill, was decided in 1954 with *Brown v. Board of Education*, which rejected the segregationist doctrine of "separate but equal". But, in 1958, under the policy of "massive resistance" led by the influential segregationist Senator Harry F. Byrd and his Byrd Organization, the Commonwealth prohibited desegregated local schools from receiving state funding.[87]

The Civil Rights Movement gained many participants in the 1960s. It achieved the moral force and support to gain passage of national legislation with the Civil Rights Act of 1964 and the Voting Rights Act of 1965. In 1964 the United States Supreme Court ordered Prince Edward County and others to integrate schools.[88] In 1967, the Court also struck down the state's ban on interracial marriage. From 1969 to 1971, state legislators under Governor Mills Godwin rewrote the constitution, after goals such as the repeal of Jim Crow laws had been achieved. In 1989, Douglas Wilder became the first African American elected as governor in the United States.[89]

New economic forces also changed the Commonwealth. In 1926, Dr. W.A.R. Goodwin, rector of Williamsburg's Bruton Parish Church, began restoration of colonial-era buildings in the historic district with financial backing of John D. Rockefeller, Jr.; their work led to the development of Colonial Williamsburg, the state's most popular tourism site.[90] World War II and the Cold War led to the expansion of national defense government programs housed in offices in Northern Virginia near Washington, D.C., and correlative population growth.[91] Among the federal developments was the Pentagon, built during WWII as the headquarters for the Department of Defense. It was one of the targets of the September 11 attacks; 189 people died at the site when a jet passenger plane crashed into the building.[92]

Cities and towns

The population of the Hampton Roads area is over 1.6 million.

Virginia is divided into 95 counties and 39 independent cities, which both operate the same way since independent cities are considered to be county-equivalent.[93] This method of treating cities and counties equally is unique to Virginia, with only three other independent cities in the United States outside Virginia.[94] Virginia limits the authority of cities and counties to countermand laws expressly allowed by the Virginia General Assembly under what is known as Dillon's Rule.[95] In addition to independent cities, there are also incorporated *towns* which operate under their own governments, but are part of a county. Finally there are hundreds of unincorporated communities within the counties. Virginia does not have any further political subdivisions, such as villages or townships.

Virginia has 11 Metropolitan Statistical Areas; Northern Virginia, Hampton Roads, and Richmond-Petersburg are the three most populous. Richmond is the capital of Virginia, and its metropolitan area has a population of over 1.2 million.[96] As of 2010, Virginia Beach is the most populous city in the Commonwealth, with Norfolk and Chesapeake second and third, respectively.[97] Norfolk forms the urban core of the Hampton Roads metropolitan area, which has a population over 1.6 million people and is the site of the world's largest naval base, Naval Station Norfolk.[96] [98] Suffolk, which includes a portion of the Great Dismal Swamp, is the largest city by area at 429.1 square miles (1111 km^2).[99]

Fairfax County is the most populous locality in Virginia, with over one million residents, although that does not include its county seat Fairfax, which is one of the independent cities.[100] Fairfax County has a major urban business and shopping center in Tysons Corner, Virginia's largest office market.[101] Neighboring Loudoun County, with the county seat at Leesburg, is both the fastest-growing county in Virginia and has the highest median household income ($114,204) in the country as of 2010.[102] Arlington County, the smallest self-governing county in the United States by land area, is an urban community organized as a county.[103] The Roanoke area, with an estimated population of 300,399, is the largest Metropolitan Statistical Area in western Virginia.[104]

Demographics

Historical populations		
Census	**Pop.**	**%±**
1790	691737	—
1800	807557	16.7%
1810	877683	8.7%
1820	938261	6.9%
1830	1044054	11.3%
1840	1025227	−1.8%
1850	1119348	9.2%
1860	1219630	9.0%
1870	1225163	0.5%
1880	1512565	23.5%
1890	1655980	9.5%
1900	1854184	12.0%
1910	2061612	11.2%
1920	2309187	12.0%
1930	2421851	4.9%
1940	2677773	10.6%
1950	3318680	23.9%
1960	3966949	19.5%
1970	4648494	17.2%
1980	5346818	15.0%
1990	6187358	15.7%
2000	7078515	14.4%
2010	8001024	13.0%

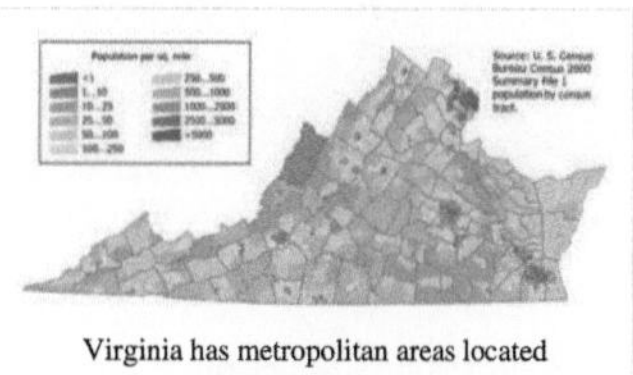

Virginia has metropolitan areas located throughout the state.

As of the 2010 census, Virginia had a population of 8,001,024 which is an increase of 118,434, or about 1.5%, from the prior year's estimate and an increase of 922,509, or 13%, since 2000.[2] This includes an increase from net migration of 314,832 people into the Commonwealth. Immigration from outside the United States resulted in a net increase of 159,627 people, and migration within the country produced a net increase of 155,205 people.[105] As of the same census, the state's population was 64.8% Non-Hispanic White, 19.4% African-American, 7.9% Hispanic or Latino (of any race), 5.5% Asian, 0.4% American Indian and Alaska Native, 0.1% Native Hawaiian and other Pacific Islander.[106] The center of population is located in Goochland County outside of Richmond.[107]

English was passed as the Commonwealth's official language by statutes in 1981 and again in 1996, though the status is not mandated by the Constitution of Virginia.[108] English is the only language spoken by 6,245,517 (86.7%) Virginians, though it is spoken "very well" by an additional 570,638 (7.9%) for a total of 94.6% of the Commonwealth. Among speakers of other languages, Spanish is the most common with 424,381 (5.9%). 226,911

(3.2%) speak Asian and Pacific Islander languages, including Korean, Vietnamese, and Filipino.[109]

Religion

Religion (2008)	
Christian[110]	76%
Baptist	27%
Roman Catholic	11%
Methodist	8%
Lutheran	2%
Other Christian	28%
Buddhism	1%
Hinduism	1%
Judaism	1%
Islam	0.5%
Unaffiliated	18%

Virginia is predominantly Christian and Protestant; Baptists are the largest single group with 27% of the population as of 2008.[110] Baptist denominational groups in Virginia include the Baptist General Association of Virginia, with about 1,400 member churches, which supports both the Southern Baptist Convention and the moderate Cooperative Baptist Fellowship; and the Southern Baptist Conservatives of Virginia with more than 500 affiliated churches, which supports the Southern Baptist Convention.[111] [112] Roman Catholics are the second-largest religious group, and the group which grew the most in the 1990s.[113] [114] The Roman Catholic Diocese of Arlington includes most of Northern Virginia's Catholic churches, while the Diocese of Richmond covers the rest.

Christ Church in Alexandria was frequented by George Washington and Robert E. Lee.

The Virginia Conference is the regional body of the United Methodist Church and the Virginia Synod is responsible for the congregations of the Lutheran Church. Presbyterians, Pentecostals, Congregationalists, and Episcopalians each composed 1–3% of the population as of 2001.[115] The Episcopal Diocese of Virginia, Southern Virginia, and Southwestern Virginia support the various Episcopal churches.

In November 2006, 15 conservative Episcopal churches voted to split from the Diocese of Virginia over the ordination of openly gay bishops and clergy in other dioceses of the Episcopal Church; these churches continue to claim affiliation with the larger Anglican Communion through other bodies outside the United States. Though Virginia law allows parishioners to determine their church's affiliation, the diocese claims the secessionist churches' properties. The resulting property law case is a test for Episcopal churches nationwide.[116]

Among other religions, adherents of The Church of Jesus Christ of Latter-day Saints constitute 1% of the population, with 190 congregations in Virginia as of 2010.[117] Fairfax Station is the site of the Ekoji Buddhist Temple, of the Jodo Shinshu school, and the Hindu Durga Temple. While the state's Jewish population is small, organized Jewish sites date to 1789 with Congregation Beth Ahabah.[118] Muslims are a growing religious group throughout the Commonwealth through immigration.[119] Megachurches in the Commonwealth include Thomas Road Baptist Church, Immanuel Bible Church, and McLean Bible Church.[120] Several Christian universities are also based in the state, including Regent University, Liberty University, and Lynchburg College.

Economy

The Department of Defense is headquartered in Arlington at The Pentagon, the world's largest office building.[121]

While Virginia is an employment-at-will state,[122] its economy has diverse sources of income, including local and federal government, military, farming and business. Virginia has 4.1 million civilian workers, and one-third of the jobs are in the service sector.[123] [124] The unemployment rate was 6.3% as of April 2011.[125] The Gross Domestic Product of Virginia was $424 billion in 2010.[126] According to the Bureau of Economic Analysis, Virginia had the most counties in the top 100 wealthiest in the United States based upon median income in 2007.[127]

Virginia has the highest concentration of technology workers of any state.[128] Computer chips became the state's highest-grossing export in 2006, surpassing its traditional top exports of coal and tobacco combined.[8] Northern Virginia, once considered the state's dairy capital, now hosts software, communication technology, and consulting companies, particularly in the Dulles Technology Corridor. Northern Virginia's data centers currently carry more than 50% of the nation's internet traffic, and by 2012 Dominion Power expects that 10% of all its electricity in Northern Virginia will be used by data centers.[129] Loudoun and Fairfax counties in Northern Virginia have the highest and second highest median household income, respectively, of all counties in the United States as of 2011.[102]

Virginia companies received the fourth-highest amount of venture capital funding in the first half of 2011 after California, Massachusetts, and New York.[130] In 2009, *Forbes Magazine* named Virginia the best state in the nation for business for the fourth year in a row,[131] while CNBC named it the top state for business in 2007, 2009, and 2011.[132] Virginia has 20 Fortune 500 companies, ranking the state eighth nationwide.[133]

Virginia has the highest defense spending of any state per capita, providing the Commonwealth with around 900,000 jobs, and 10% of all U.S. federal procurement money is spent in Virginia.[134] [135] Virginia has over 800,000 veterans, more than any other state, and is second to California in total Department of Defense employees.[135] [136] Many Virginians work for federal agencies in Northern Virginia, which include the Central Intelligence Agency and the Department of Defense, as well as the National Science Foundation, the United States Geological Survey and the United States Patent and Trademark Office. Many others work for government contractors, including defense and security firms, which hold more than 15,000 federal contracts.[137] The Hampton Roads area has the largest concentration of military bases and facilities of any metropolitan area in the world. The largest of the bases is Naval Station Norfolk.[98]

Ocean tourism is an important sector of Virginia Beach's economy.

Agriculture occupies 24% of the land in Virginia. As of 2007, about 357,000 Virginian jobs were in agriculture, with over 47,000 farms, averaging 171 acres (0.27 sq mi; 0.69 km^2), in a total farmland area of 8.1 million acres (12,656 sq mi; 32,780 km^2). Though agriculture has declined significantly since 1960 when there were twice as many farms, it remains the largest single industry in Virginia.[138] Tomatoes surpassed soy as the most profitable crop in Virginia in 2006, with peanuts and hay as other agricultural products.[139] Although it is no longer the primary crop, Virginia is still the fifth-largest producer of tobacco nationwide.[140] Eastern oyster harvests are an important part of the Chesapeake Bay economy, but declining oyster populations from disease, pollution, and overfishing have diminished catches.[141] Wineries and vineyards in the Northern Neck and along the Blue Ridge Mountains also have begun to generate income and attract tourists.[142]

Virginia collects personal income tax in five income brackets, ranging from 3.0% to 5.75%. The state sales and use tax rate is 4%, while the tax rate on food is 1.5%. There is an additional 1% local tax, for a total of a 5% combined sales tax on most Virginia purchases and 2.5% on most food.[143] Virginia's property tax is set and collected at the local government level and varies throughout the Commonwealth. Real estate is also taxed at the local level based on 100% of fair market value. Tangible personal property also is taxed at the local level and is based on a percentage or percentages of original cost.[144]

Culture

Virginia's historic culture was popularized and spread across America and the South by figures such as George Washington, Thomas Jefferson, and Robert E. Lee. Their homes in Virginia represent the birthplace of America and the South. Modern Virginia culture has many sources, and is part of the culture of the Southern United States.[145] [146] The Smithsonian Institution divides Virginia into nine cultural regions.[147] The Piedmont region is one of the most famous for its dialect's strong influence on Southern American English. While a more homogenized American English is found in urban areas, various accents are also used, including the Tidewater accent, the Old Virginia accent, and the anachronistic Elizabethan of Tangier Island.[148] [149]

Colonial Virginian culture, language, and style are reenacted in Williamsburg.

Literature in Virginia often deals with the state's extensive and sometimes troubled past. The works of Pulitzer Prize winner Ellen Glasgow often dealt with social inequalities and the role of women in her culture.[150] Glasgow's peer and close friend James Branch Cabell wrote extensively about the changing position of gentry in the Reconstruction era, and challenged its moral code with *Jurgen, A Comedy of Justice*.[151] William Styron approached history in works such as *The Confessions of Nat Turner* and *Sophie's Choice*.[152] Tom Wolfe has occasionally dealt with his southern heritage in bestsellers like *I Am Charlotte Simmons*.[153] Virginia also names a state Poet Laureate, currently Kelly Cherry of Halifax County, who will serve until 2012.[154]

Besides the general cuisine of the Southern United States, Virginia maintains its own particular traditions. Virginia wine is made in many parts of the state.[142] Smithfield ham, sometimes called "Virginia ham", is a type of country ham which is protected by state law, and can only be produced in the town of Smithfield.[155] Virginia furniture and architecture are typical of American colonial architecture. Thomas Jefferson and many of the state's early leaders favored the Neoclassical architecture style, leading to its use for important state buildings. The Pennsylvania Dutch and their style can also be found in parts of the state.[156]

Fine and performing arts

Though rich in cultural heritage, Virginia ranks near the bottom of U.S. states in terms of public spending on the arts, at nearly half of the national average.[157] The state government does fund some institutions, including the Virginia Museum of Fine Arts and the Science Museum of Virginia. Other museums include the popular Steven F. Udvar-Hazy Center of the National Air and Space Museum and the Chrysler Museum of Art.[158] Besides these sites, many open-air museums are located in the Commonwealth, such as Colonial Williamsburg, the Frontier Culture Museum, and various historic battlefields.[159] The Virginia Foundation for the Humanities works to improve the Commonwealth's civic, cultural, and intellectual life.[160]

The Meadow Pavilion is one of the theaters at Wolf Trap National Park for the Performing Arts.

Theaters and venues in the Commonwealth are found both in the cities and suburbs. Wolf Trap National Park for the Performing Arts is located in Vienna and is the only national park intended for use as a performing arts center.[161] The Harrison Opera House, in Norfolk, is home of the Virginia Opera. The Virginia Symphony Orchestra operates in and around Hampton Roads.[162] Resident and touring theater troupes operate from the American Shakespeare Center in Staunton.[163] The Barter Theatre in Abingdon won the first ever Regional Theatre Tony Award in 1948, while the Signature Theatre in Arlington won it in 2009. There's also a Children's Theater of Virginia, Theatre IV, which is the second largest touring troupe nationwide.[164] Virginia has launched many award-winning traditional musical artists and internationally successful popular music acts, as well as Hollywood actors.[1] Notable performance venues include The Birchmere, the Landmark Theater, and Jiffy Lube Live.[165]

Festivals

Many counties and localities host county fairs and festivals. The Virginia State Fair is held at the Meadow Event Park every September. Also in September is the Neptune Festival in Virginia Beach, which celebrates the city, the waterfront, and regional artists. Norfolk's Harborfest, in June, features boat racing and air shows.[166] Fairfax County also sponsors Celebrate Fairfax! with popular and traditional music performances.[167] The Virginia Lake Festival is held during the third weekend in July in Clarksville.[168] Wolf Trap hosts the Wolf Trap Opera Company, which produces an opera festival every summer.[161]

The annual Chincoteague Pony Swim features over 200 wild ponies swimming across the Assateague Channel into Chincoteague.

On the Eastern Shore island of Chincoteague the annual Pony Swim & Auction of feral Chincoteague ponies at the end of July is a unique local tradition expanded into a week-long carnival. The Shenandoah Apple Blossom Festival is a six-day festival held annually in Winchester that includes parades and bluegrass concerts. The Old Time Fiddlers' Convention in Galax, begun in 1935, is one of the oldest and largest such events worldwide. Two important film festivals, the Virginia Film Festival and the VCU French Film Festival, are held annually in Charlottesville and Richmond, respectively.[166]

Media

USA Today, the nation's most circulated newspaper, has its headquarters in McLean.

The Hampton Roads area is the 43rd-largest media market in the United States as ranked by Nielsen Media Research, while the Richmond-Petersburg area is 57th and Roanoke-Lynchburg is 66th as of 2010.[169] Northern Virginia is part of the much larger Washington, D.C. media market.

There are 36 television stations in Virginia, representing each major U.S. network, part of 42 stations which serve Virginia viewers.[170] More than 720 FCC-licensed FM radio stations broadcast in Virginia, with about 300 such AM stations.[171] [172] The nationally available Public Broadcasting Service (PBS) is headquartered in Arlington. Independent PBS affiliates exist throughout Virginia, and the Arlington PBS member station WETA-TV produces programs such as the *PBS NewsHour* and *Washington Week*.

The most circulated native newspapers in the Commonwealth are Norfolk's *The Virginian-Pilot* (156,968 daily subscribers), the *Richmond Times-Dispatch* (118,489), *The Roanoke Times* (75,740), and Newport News' *Daily Press* (63,366), as of 2010.[173] Several Washington, D.C. papers are based in Northern Virginia, such as *The Washington Examiner* and *Politico*. The paper with the nation's widest circulation, *USA Today*, with 1.83 million daily subscriptions, is headquartered in McLean.[174] Besides traditional forms of media, Virginia is the home base for telecommunication companies such as Voxant and XO Communications. In Northern Virginia, The Washington Post is the dominant newspaper, since Northern VA is located in the Washington, DC metropolitan area.

Education

The University of Virginia, a World Heritage Site, was founded by President Thomas Jefferson.[175]

Virginia's educational system consistently ranks in the top ten states on the U.S. Department of Education's National Assessment of Educational Progress, with Virginia students outperforming the average in all subject areas and grade levels tested.[176] The 2011 *Quality Counts* report ranked Virginia's K–12 education fourth best in the country.[177] All school divisions must adhere to educational standards set forth by the Virginia Department of Education, which maintains an assessment and accreditation regime known as the Standards of Learning to ensure accountability.[178] In 2010, 85% of high school students graduated on-time after four years.[179] Between 2000 and 2008, school enrollment increased 5%, the number of teachers 21%.[180]

Public K–12 schools in Virginia are generally operated by the counties and cities, and not by the state. As of April 2011, a total of 1,267,063 students were enrolled in 1,873 local and regional schools in the Commonwealth, including three charter schools, and an additional 109 alternative and special education centers across 132 school divisions.[181] [182] Besides the general public schools in Virginia, there are Governor's Schools and selective magnet schools. The Governor's Schools are a collection of more than 40 regional high schools and summer programs intended for gifted students.[183] The Virginia Council for Private Education oversees the regulation of 320 state accredited and 130 non-accredited private schools.[184] [185] An additional 24,682 students receive homeschooling.[186]

As of 2011, there are 176 colleges and universities in Virginia.[187] In the *U.S. News and World Report* ranking of public colleges, the University of Virginia is second and The College of William & Mary is sixth.[188] [189] Virginia

Commonwealth University is ranked the top public graduate school in fine arts, while James Madison University has been recognized as the top regional public master's program in The South since 1993.[190] [191] The Virginia Military Institute is the oldest state military college and a top ranked public liberal arts college.[192] [193] George Mason University is the largest university in Virginia with over 32,000 students.[194] Virginia Tech and Virginia State University are the state's land-grant universities. Virginia also operates 23 community colleges on 40 campuses serving over 260,000 students.[195] There are 129 private institutions, including Washington and Lee University, Hampden–Sydney College, Emory & Henry College, Roanoke College, and the University of Richmond.[187]

Health

The A.D. Williams Clinic and West Hospital at VCU Medical Center in Richmond

Virginia has a mixed health record, and is ranked as the 22nd overall healthiest state according to the 2010 United Health Foundation's Health Rankings.[196] Virginia also ranks 21st among the states in the rate of premature deaths, 7,104 per 100,000. In 2008, Virginia reached its lowest ever rate of infant mortality, at 6.7 deaths per 1,000.[197] There are however racial and social health disparities, with African Americans experiencing 27.9% more premature deaths than whites, while 12.7% of Virginians lack any health insurance.[196] According to the Centers for Disease Control and Prevention's 2009 survey, 25.5% of Virginians are obese and another 35.1% are overweight. 78.1% of residents claim to have exercised once in the past three months.[198] [199] About 30% of Virginia's 10- to 17-year-olds are overweight or obese.[200] Virginia banned smoking in bars and restaurants in January 2010.[201] 19% of Virginians smoke tobacco.[196]

There are 89 hospitals in Virginia listed with the United States Department of Health and Human Services.[202] Notable examples include Inova Fairfax Hospital, the largest hospital in the Washington Metropolitan Area, and the VCU Medical Center, located on the medical campus of Virginia Commonwealth University. The University of Virginia Medical Center, part of the University of Virginia Health System, is highly ranked in endocrinology according to *U.S.News & World Report*.[203] Sentara Norfolk General Hospital, part of the Hampton Roads based Sentara Health System and a teaching institution of Eastern Virginia Medical School, was the site of the first successful in-vitro fertilization birth.[204] [205] Virginia has a ratio of 124 primary care physicians per 10,000 residents, which is the 13th highest nationally.[196] Virginia was one of five states to receive a perfect score in disaster preparedness according to a 2008 report by the Trust for America's Health, based on criteria such as detecting pathogens and distributing vaccines and medical supplies.[206]

Transportation

The Virginia Railway Express runs commuter lines in Northern Virginia.

Because of the 1932 Byrd Road Act, the state government controls most of Virginia's roads, instead of a local county authority as is usual in other states.[207] As of 2011, the Virginia Department of Transportation owns and operates 57867 miles (93128 km) of the total 70105 miles (km) of roads in the state, making it the third largest state highway system in the United States.[208] Although the Washington Metropolitan Area, which includes Northern Virginia, has the second worst traffic in the nation, Virginia as a whole has the 21st-lowest congestion and the average commute time is 26.9 minutes.[209] [210]

Virginia has Amtrak passenger rail service along several corridors, and Virginia Railway Express (VRE) maintains two commuter lines into Washington, D.C. from Fredericksburg and Manassas. VRE is one of the nation's fastest growing commuter rail services, handling nearly 20,000 passengers a day.[211] The Washington Metro rapid transit system serves Northern Virginia as far west as communities along I-66 in Fairfax County, with expansion plans to reach Tysons Corner by 2013, and Loudoun County by 2017.[212] Major freight railroads in Virginia include Norfolk Southern and CSX Transportation. Commuter buses include the Fairfax Connector and the Shenandoah Valley Commuter Bus. The Virginia Department of Transportation operates several free ferries throughout Virginia, the most notable being the Jamestown-Scotland ferry which crosses the James River in Surry County.[213]

Virginia has five major airports: Washington Dulles International handling over 23 million passengers a year, Reagan Washington National, Norfolk International serving the Hampton Roads area, Richmond International, and Newport News/Williamsburg International Airport. Several other airports offer limited commercial passenger service, and sixty-six public airports serve the state's aviation needs.[214] The Virginia Port Authority's main seaports are those in Hampton Roads, which carried 17726251 short tons (t) of bulk cargo in 2007, the sixth most of United States ports.[215] The Eastern Shore of Virginia is the site of Wallops Flight Facility, a rocket testing center owned by NASA, and the Mid-Atlantic Regional Spaceport, a commercial spaceport.[216] [217] Space tourism is also offered through Vienna-based Space Adventures.[218]

Law and government

In colonial Virginia, free men elected the lower house of the legislature, called the House of Burgesses, which together with the Governor's Council, made the "General Assembly". Founded in 1619, the Virginia General Assembly is still in existence as the oldest legislature in the Western Hemisphere.[219] The modern government is ranked by the Pew Center on the States with an A– in terms of its efficiency, effectiveness, and infrastructure. This is the second time Virginia received the highest grade in the nation, which it shares with two others.[7]

The Virginia State Capitol, designed by Thomas Jefferson and begun by Governor Patrick Henry in 1785, is home to the Virginia General Assembly.

Since 1971, the government has functioned under the seventh Constitution of Virginia, which provides for a strong legislature and a unified judicial system. Similar to the federal structure, the government is divided in three branches: legislative, executive, and judicial. The legislature is the General Assembly, a bicameral body whose 100-member House of Delegates and 40-member Senate write the laws for the Commonwealth. The Assembly is stronger than the executive, as it selects judges and justices. The Governor and Lieutenant Governor are elected every four years in separate elections. Incumbent governors cannot run for re-election, however the Lieutenant Governor and Attorney General can, and governors may serve non-consecutive terms.[220] The judicial system, the oldest in America, consists of a hierarchy from the Supreme Court of Virginia and the Court of Appeals of Virginia to the lower general district and circuit courts.[221]

The Code of Virginia is the statutory law, and consists of the codified legislation of the General Assembly. The Virginia State Police is the largest law enforcement agency in Virginia. The Virginia Capitol Police is the oldest police department in the United States.[222] The Virginia National Guard consists of 7,500 soldiers in the Virginia Army National Guard and 1,200 airmen in the Virginia Air National Guard.[223] Since the resumption of capital punishment in Virginia in 1982, 107 people have been executed, the second highest number in the nation.[224] The "total crime risk" is 28% lower than the national average.[225] Since Virginia ended prisoner parole in 1995, the rate of recidivism has fallen to 28.3%, among the lowest nationwide.[226]

Politics

Over the 20th century, Virginia shifted from a largely rural, politically Southern and conservative state to a more urbanized, pluralistic, and politically moderate environment. Up until the 1970s, Virginia was a racially divided single-party state dominated by the Byrd Organization.[227] The legacy of slavery in the state effectively disfranchised African Americans until after passage of civil rights legislation in the mid-1960s.[228] Enfranchisement and immigration of other groups, especially Hispanics, have placed growing importance on minority voting.[229] Regional differences play a large part in Virginia politics.[230] Rural southern and western areas moved to support the Republican Party in response to its "southern strategy", while urban and growing suburban areas, including much of Northern Virginia, form the Democratic Party base.[231] [232] Democratic support also persists in union-influenced parts of Southwest Virginia, college towns such as Charlottesville and Blacksburg, and the southeastern Black Belt Region.[233]

Jim Webb speaks at a Richmond rally with former Governors Mark Warner, Tim Kaine, and Douglas Wilder, President Barack Obama, and others.

Political party strength in Virginia has likewise been in flux. In the 2007 state elections, Democrats regained control of the State Senate, and narrowed the Republican majority in the House of Delegates to eight seats.[234] Yet elections in 2009 resulted in the election of Republican Robert McDonnell as governor by a 17 point margin, the election of a Republican Lieutenant Governor and Attorney General, as well as Republican gains of six seats in the House of Delegates.[235] In 2011, the Republican caucus took over two-thirds of the seats in the House of Delegates, and a majority of the Senate based on the Lieutenant Governor Bill Bolling as the tie-breaker.[236] State election seasons traditionally start with the annual Shad Planking event in Wakefield.[237]

In federal elections since 2006, both parties have seen success. In the 2006 Senate election, Democrat Jim Webb won on a populist platform over the Republican incumbent following a very close race.[238] The party took both U.S. Senate seats with the election of former Governor Mark Warner to replace retiring Republican John Warner.[239] Virginia, which has 13 electoral votes, was won by Democrat Barack Obama in 2008, after being won by Republican candidates in the previous ten presidential elections.[240] In the 2010 elections, Republicans picked up three House seats from Democrats. Of the state's 11 seats in the U.S. House of Representatives, Republicans hold eight and Democrats hold three. Virginia may be considered a "swing state" in future presidential elections.[6]

Sports

The Virginia Tech Hokies football team has the third longest bowl game streak in the nation.[241]

Virginia is the most populous U.S. state without a major professional sports league franchise.[242] The reasons for this include the lack of any dominant city or market within the state and the proximity of teams in Washington, D.C.[243] Virginia has several minor league clubs, especially in baseball and soccer, and the Virginia Destroyers are the 2011 champions of the United Football League.[244] Additionally, the Washington Redskins have Redskins Park, their headquarters and training facility, in Ashburn and the Washington Capitals train at Kettler Capitals Iceplex in Ballston.[245] Virginia has many professional caliber golf courses including the Greg Norman course at Lansdowne Resort and Kingsmill Resort, home of the Michelob ULTRA Open. NASCAR currently schedules Sprint Cup races on two tracks in Virginia: Martinsville Speedway and Richmond International Raceway. Current Virginia drivers in the series include Jeff Burton, Denny Hamlin, and Elliott Sadler.[246]

The Washington Nationals and Baltimore Orioles also have followings due to their proximity, and both are broadcast in the state on MASN.[247] When the New York Mets ended their long affiliation with the Norfolk Tides in 2007, the Orioles adopted the minor league club as their top level (AAA) minor league affiliate.[248] The San Francisco Giants' AA team, the Richmond Flying Squirrels, began play at The Diamond in 2010, replacing the AAA Richmond Braves, who relocated after 2008.[249] Additionally, the Nationals, Boston Red Sox, Seattle Mariners, Chicago White Sox, and Atlanta Braves also have Single-A and Rookie-level farm teams in Virginia.[250]

Virginia does not allow state appropriated funds to be used for either operational or capital expenses for intercollegiate athletics.[251] Despite this, both the Virginia Cavaliers and Virginia Tech Hokies have been able to field competitive teams in the Atlantic Coast Conference and maintain modern facilities. Their rivalry is followed statewide. Several other universities compete in NCAA Division I, particularly in the Colonial Athletic Association. Three historically black schools compete in the Division II Central Intercollegiate Athletic Association, and two others compete in the Division I Mid-Eastern Athletic Conference. Several smaller schools compete in the Old Dominion Athletic Conference and the USA South Athletic Conference of NCAA Division III. The NCAA currently holds its Division III championships in football, men's basketball, volleyball and softball in Salem.[252]

State symbols

The Virginia welcome sign at the Virginia welcome center on I-95 employs the state bird, the cardinal, and the state tree and flower, the dogwood.

The state nickname is its oldest symbol, though it has never been made official by law. Virginia was given the title "Dominion" by King Charles II of England at the time of The Restoration, because it had remained loyal to the crown during the English Civil War, and the present moniker, "Old Dominion" is a reference to that title. The other nickname, "Mother of Presidents", is also historic, as eight Virginians have served as President of the United States, including four of the first five.[1]

The state's motto, *Sic Semper Tyrannis*, translates from Latin as "Thus Always to Tyrants", and is used on the state seal, which is then used on the flag. While the seal was designed in 1776, and the flag was first used in the 1830s, both were made official in 1930.[1] The majority of the other symbols were made official in the late 20th century.[253] The Virginia reel is among the square dances classified as the state dance.[15] Virginia currently has no state song. In 1940, Virginia made "Carry Me Back to Old Virginny" the state song, but it was retired in 1997 and reclassified as the state song emeritus.[254] Various alternatives, including a version of "Oh Shenandoah", have met with resistance in the Virginia House of Delegates.[255]

- Mammal: Virginia Big-Eared Bat
- Beverage: Milk
- Boat: Chesapeake Bay deadrise
- Bird: Cardinal
- Dance: Square dancing
- Dog: American Foxhound
- Fish: Brook trout, Striped bass
- Flower/Tree: Dogwood
- Fossil: Chesapecten jeffersonius
- Insect: Tiger swallowtail
- Motto: Sic Semper Tyrannis
- Nickname: The Old Dominion
- Shell: Eastern oyster
- Slogan: Virginia is for Lovers
- Tartan: Virginia Quadricentennial

See also

- National Register of Historic Places listings in Virginia

References

[1] "Factpack" (http://legis.state.va.us/1_cap_class/class_media/4_5_pdfs/factpack-1.pdf) (PDF). Virginia General Assembly. January 11, 2007. . Retrieved October 14, 2008.

[2] "Virginia Sees Another Decade of Double-Digit Growth" (http://www.wusa9.com/news/local/story.aspx?storyid=126835). *WUSA 9*. Associated Press. December 21, 2010. . Retrieved April 12, 2011.

[3] "Median household income in the past 12 months (in 2007 inflation-adjusted dollars)" (http://factfinder.census.gov/servlet/STTable?_bm=y&-geo_id=04000US51&-qr_name=ACS_2008_3YR_G00_S1901&-ds_name=ACS_2008_3YR_G00_). *American Community Survey*. United States Census Bureau. 2007. . Retrieved September 2, 2008.

[4] "Elevations and Distances in the United States" (http://egsc.usgs.gov/isb/pubs/booklets/elvadist/elvadist.html). United States Geological Survey. 2001. . Retrieved October 24, 2011.

[5] Elevation adjusted to North American Vertical Datum of 1988.

[6] Balz, Dan (October 12, 2007). "Painting America Purple" (http://blog.washingtonpost.com/44/2007/10/12/the_purpling_of_america.html). *The Washington Post*. . Retrieved November 24, 2007.

[7] Somashekhar, Sandhya (March 4, 2008). "Government Takes Top Honors in Efficiency" (http://www.washingtonpost.com/wp-dyn/content/story/2008/03/03/ST2008030303550.html). *The Washington Post*. . Retrieved March 11, 2008.

[8] Richards, Gregory (February 24, 2007). "Computer chips now lead Virginia exports" (http://web.archive.org/web/20070310155937/http://content.hamptonroads.com/story.cfm?story=120082&ran=25886). *The Virginian-Pilot*. Archived from the original (http://content.hamptonroads.com/story.cfm?story=120082&ran=25886) on 2007-03-10. . Retrieved September 29, 2008.

[9] "2000 Census of Population and Housing" (http://www.census.gov/prod/cen2000/phc3-us-pt1.pdf) (PDF). *United States Census Bureau*. April 2004. p. 71. . Retrieved November 3, 2009.

[10] "Supreme Court Rules for Virginia in Potomac Conflict" (http://nsglc.olemiss.edu/SandBar/SandBar2/2.4supreme.htm). *The Sea Grant Law Center*. University of Mississippi. 2003. . Retrieved November 24, 2007.

[11] Hubbard, Jr. 2009, p. 140

[12] "Fact Sheet 102–98 – The Chesapeake Bay: Geologic Product of Rising Sea Level" (http://pubs.usgs.gov/fs/fs102-98/). United States Geological Survey. November 18, 1998. . Retrieved August 24, 2009.

[13] Burnham & Burnham 2004, pp. 7, 56–57

[14] "Rivers and Watersheds" (http://web.wm.edu/geology/virginia/rivers/rivers.html). *The Geology of Virginia*. College of William and Mary. February 23, 2007. . Retrieved April 11, 2008.

[15] The Encyclopedia of Virginia 1999, pp. 2–15

[16] Pazzaglia 2006, pp. 135–138

[17] "Virginia's Agricultural Resources" (http://www.deq.state.va.us/vanaturally/guide/agriculture.html). *Natural Resource Education Guide*. Virginia Department of Environmental Quality. January 21, 2008. . Retrieved February 8, 2008.

[18] Burnham & Burnham 2004, p. 277

[19] "Physiographic Regions of Virginia" (http://web.wm.edu/geology/virginia/provinces/phys_regions.html). *The Geology of Virginia*. College of William and Mary. February 16, 2007. . Retrieved April 7, 2008.

[20] Palmer 1998, pp. 49–51

[21] Heinemann et al. 2007, p. 3

[22] "Caves" (http://www.dmme.virginia.gov/DMR3/dmrpdfs/CAVES.pdf) (PDF). Virginia Department of Mines, Minerals and Energy. July 2008. . Retrieved August 24, 2009.

[23] "Largest Earthquake in Virginia" (http://earthquake.usgs.gov/regional/states/events/1897_05_31.php). United States Geological Survey. January 25, 2008. . Retrieved April 12, 2008.

[24] "Magnitude 5.8 - Virginia" (http://earthquake.usgs.gov/earthquakes/recenteqsww/Quakes/se082311a.php#summary). United States Geological Survey. August 23, 2011. . Retrieved November 13, 2011.

[25] "Coal" (http://www.dmme.virginia.gov/DMR3/coal.shtml). Virginia Department of Mines, Minerals, and Energy. 2006. . Retrieved August 24, 2009.

[26] "About DMME" (http://www.dmme.virginia.gov/aboutus.shtml). Virginia Department of Mines, Minerals and Energy. 2006. . Retrieved September 11, 2009.

[27] Burnham & Burnham 2004, pp. 1–3

[28] Hayden, Bruce P.; Michaels, Patrick J. (January 20, 2000). "Virginia's Climate" (http://climate.virginia.edu/description.htm). *Department of Environmental Sciences*. University of Virginia. . Retrieved October 20, 2008.

[29] "Thunderstorms and Lightening" (http://www.vaemergency.com/news/history/thunderstorms-lightening). *Virginia Department of Emergency Management*. April 2, 2001. . Retrieved November 26, 2011.

[30] "The Natural Communities of Virginia" (http://www.dcr.virginia.gov/natural_heritage/ncoverview.shtml). Virginia Department of Conservation and Recreation. 2006. . Retrieved April 12, 2008.

[31] Ricketts, Lauryn (February 7, 2008). "Tornadoes DO happen in Virginia!" (http://www.tv3winchester.com/blogs/laurynrickettsblog/15421801.html). TV3 Winchester. . Retrieved February 13, 2009.
[32] "Advisory 01/07: The Hot Get Hotter? Urban Warming and Air Quality" (http://web.archive.org/web/20020922182906/http://climate.virginia.edu/advisory/2001/ad01-07.htm). University of Virginia Climatology Office. Archived from the original (http://climate.virginia.edu/advisory/2001/ad01-07.htm) on 2002-09-22. . Retrieved July 30, 2007.
[33] "Report Card: Virginia" (http://www.stateoftheair.org/2011/states/virginia/). *State of the Air: 2011*. American Lung Association. April 27, 2011. . Retrieved May 10, 2011.
[34] "Fairfax County Residents Can Play Their Part to Reduce Air Pollution" (http://www.fairfaxcounty.gov/news/2004/04145.htm). Fairfax County, Virginia. May 26, 2004. . Retrieved September 29, 2008.
[35] Fahrenthold, David A. (June 25, 2008). "Debating Coal's Cost in Rural Va." (http://www.washingtonpost.com/wp-dyn/content/story/2008/06/25/ST2008062500042.html). *The Washington Post*. . Retrieved November 15, 2008.
[36] "Virginia's Forest Resources" (http://www.deq.virginia.gov/vanaturally/guide/forests.html). *Natural Resource Education Guide*. Virginia Department of Environmental Quality. January 21, 2008. . Retrieved February 8, 2008.
[37] "Shenandoah National Park — Forests" (http://www.nps.gov/shen/naturescience/forests.htm). National Park Service. July 25, 2006. . Retrieved September 10, 2007.
[38] Carroll & Miller 2002, pp. xi–xii
[39] "Species Information: Mammals" (http://www.dgif.virginia.gov/wildlife/information/?t=2). Virginia Department of Game and Inland Fisheries. 2008. . Retrieved November 15, 2008.
[40] "Shenandoah National Park — Birds" (http://www.nps.gov/shen/naturescience/birds.htm). National Park Service. July 25, 2006. . Retrieved September 1, 2007.
[41] "Virginia Fishes" (http://www.dgif.virginia.gov/wildlife/fish/). Virginia Department of Game and Inland Fisheries. 2008. . Retrieved November 15, 2008.
[42] "Bay Biology" (http://www.chesapeakebay.net/info/baybio1.cfm). Chesapeake Bay Program. January 5, 2006. . Retrieved February 4, 2008.
[43] "Virginia" (http://www.nps.gov/state/VA/index.htm). National Park Service. 2008. . Retrieved November 29, 2008.
[44] Carroll & Miller 2002, p. 158
[45] "Park Locations" (http://www.dcr.virginia.gov/state_parks/state_park.shtml). Virginia Department of Conservation and Recreation. November 9, 2007. . Retrieved January 26, 2008.
[46] Smith 2008, pp. 152–153, 356
[47] Wallenstein 2007, pp. 406–407
[48] Kunkle, Fredrick; Vogel, Steve (May 14, 2007). "President Bush Caps Celebration Of Success in Face of Adversity" (http://www.washingtonpost.com/wp-dyn/content/article/2007/05/13/AR2007051300412.html). *The Washington Post*. . Retrieved November 11, 2009.
[49] "Virginia Military Dead Database Introduction" (http://www.lva.virginia.gov/public/guides/vmd/vmdintro.htm). *Library of Virginia*. Government of Virginia. 2009. . Retrieved April 26, 2009.
[50] Abrams 1999, p. xv
[51] Karenne Wood, ed., *The Virginia Indian Heritage Trail* (http://virginiaindians.pwnet.org/lesson_plans/Heritage Trail_2ed.pdf), Charlottesville, VA: Virginia Foundation for the Humanities, 2007.
[52] Heinemann et al. 2007, pp. 4–11
[53] Cotton, Lee (July 1999). "Powhatan Indian Lifeways" (http://www.nps.gov/jame/historyculture/powhatan-indian-lifeways.htm). National Park Service. . Retrieved June 26, 2008.
[54] Wallenstein 2007, pp. 8–9
[55] Moran 2007, p. 8
[56] Stewart 2008, p. 22
[57] Vollmann 2002, pp. 695–696
[58] Conlin 2009, pp. 30–31
[59] Gordon 2004, p. 17
[60] Hoffer 2006, p. 132
[61] Grizzard & Smith 2007, pp. 128–133
[62] "The lost colony and Jamestown droughts." (http://www.ncdc.noaa.gov/paleo/drought/drght_james.html), Stahle, D. W., M. K. Cleaveland, D. B. Blanton, M. D. Therrell, and D. A. Gay. 1998. *Science* 280:564–567.
[63] Wallenstein 2007, p. 22
[64] Hashaw 2007, pp. 76–77, 211–212, 239–240
[65] Billings, Warren (2009). *The Old Dominion in the Seventeenth Century: A Documentary History of Virginia, 1606–1700*. Pg 286–287. ISBN 1442961260.
[66] Heinemann et al. 2007, pp. 51–59
[67] Heinemann et al. 2007, pp. 76–77
[68] Anderson 2000, p. 23
[69] Anderson 2000, pp. 42–43

[70] "Signers of the Declaration (Richard Henry Lee)" (http://www.nps.gov/history/history/online_books/declaration/bio26.htm). National Park Service. April 13, 2006. . Retrieved February 2, 2008.

[71] Gutzman 2007, pp. 24–29

[72] Heinemann et al. 2007, pp. 125–133

[73] Schwartz, Stephan A. (May 2000). "George Mason: Forgotten Founder, He Conceived the Bill of Rights". *Smithsonian* (31.2): 142.

[74] Cooper 2007, p. 58

[75] Heinemann et al. 2007, pp. 131–133

[76] Wallenstein 2007, p. 104

[77] Robertson 1993, pp. 8–12

[78] Davis 2006, pp. 125, 208–210

[79] "Census Data for Year 1860" (http://mapserver.lib.virginia.edu/php/start.php?year=V1960). University of Virginia. 2007. . Retrieved April 6, 2010.

[80] Goodwin 2008, pp. 6–8

[81] Robertson 1993, p. 170

[82] Heinemann et al. 2007, pp. 249–250

[83] Morgan 1992, pp. 160–166

[84] Dailey & Gilmore Simon, pp. 90–96

[85] Wallenstein 2007, pp. 253–254

[86] Davis 2006, pp. 328–329

[87] Wallenstein 2007, pp. 340–341

[88] Wallenstein 2007, pp. 357

[89] Heinemann et al. 2007, pp. 359–366

[90] "Colonial Williamsburg" (http://www.virginia.org/ColonialWilliamsburg/). Virginia is for Lovers. August 13, 2007. . Retrieved November 24, 2007.

[91] Accordino 2000, pp. 76–78

[92] Kelly, Christopher (November 29, 2001). "Forensic feat IDs nearly all Pentagon victims" (http://www.dcmilitary.com/dcmilitary_archives/stories/112901/12279-1.shtml). Stripe. . Retrieved September 11, 2009.

[93] "County & County Equivalent Areas" (http://www.census.gov/geo/www/cob/co_metadata.html). United States Census Bureau. April 19, 2005. . Retrieved December 8, 2007.

[94] Niemeier, Bernie (September 28, 2009). "Unique structural issues make progress in Virginia difficult" (http://www.virginiabusiness.com/index.php/opinion/article/unique-structural-issues-make-progress-in-virginia-difficult/201616/). *Virginia Business*. . Retrieved October 3, 2009.

[95] "Dillon's Rule: Legal Framework for Decision Making" (http://www.virginia.edu/ien/vnrli/docs/briefs/Dillons_Rule_09.pdf). University of Virginia. . Retrieved 2010-11-22.

[96] Davis, Marc (January 31, 2008). "Chesapeake, Suffolk on track to pass neighbors in terms of population" (http://hamptonroads.com/2008/01/chesapeake-suffolk-track-pass-neighbors-terms-population). *The Virginian-Pilot*. . Retrieved October 20, 2008.

[97] "Virginia 2010 Census Redistricting Data (Public Law 94-171) Summary File" (http://factfinder2.census.gov/bkmk/table/1.0/en/DEC/10_PL/P1/0400000US51|0400000US51.16000). *United States Census Bureau*. April 1, 2010. . Retrieved May 1, 2011.

[98] "NNSY History" (http://www.navsea.navy.mil/shipyards/norfolk/History/Home.aspx). United States Navy. August 27, 2007. . Retrieved April 6, 2010.

[99] "All About Suffolk" (http://www.suffolk.va.us/community/history.html). Suffolk. February 12, 2007. . Retrieved February 19, 2008.

[100] Somashekhar, Sandhya; Gardner, Amy (July 5, 2009). "To Be or Not to Be Fairfax County?" (http://www.washingtonpost.com/wp-dyn/content/article/2009/07/04/AR2009070402623.html). *The Washington Post*. . Retrieved August 18, 2009.

[101] "Doing Business in Fairfax County" (http://www.fairfaxcountyeda.org/re_tysons.htm). Fairfax County Economic Development Authority. June 26, 2007. . Retrieved December 8, 2007.

[102] Hager, Hannah (November 12, 2010). "Loudoun named richest county in the nation, again" (http://www.loudountimes.com/index.php/news/article/loudoun_named_rich909est_c454ounty_in_the_nation/). *Loudoun Times-Mirror*. . Retrieved May 1, 2011.

[103] Battiata, Mary (November 27, 2005). "Silent Streams" (http://www.washingtonpost.com/wp-dyn/content/article/2005/11/22/AR2005112202165_pf.html). *The Washington Post*. . Retrieved April 12, 2008.

[104] "Estimates of the Population of Metropolitan and Micropolitan Statistical Areas: April 1, 2000 to July 1, 2009 (CBSA-EST2009-01)" (http://www.census.gov/popest/metro/tables/2009/CBSA-EST2009-01.csv) (CSV). *2009 Population Estimates*. United States Census Bureau. March 23, 2010. . Retrieved March 26, 2010.

[105] "State Resident Population—Components of Change: 2000 to 2007" (http://www.census.gov/compendia/statab/2009/tables/09s0015.pdf) (PDF). United States Census Bureau. December 27, 2007. . Retrieved April 6, 2010.

[106] "State & County QuickFacts: Virginia QuickFacts from the US Census Bureau" (http://quickfacts.census.gov/qfd/states/51000.html). United States Census Bureau. 2011. . Retrieved November 30, 2011.

[107] "Population and Population Centers by State" (http://www.census.gov/geo/www/cenpop/statecenters.txt) (TXT). United States Census Bureau. 2000. . Retrieved November 7, 2007.

[108] Joseph 2006, p. 63

[109] "Virginia Selected Social Characteristics in the United States" (http://factfinder.census.gov/servlet/ADPTable?_bm=y&-qr_name=ACS_2007_1YR_G00_DP2&-geo_id=04000US51). United States Census Bureau. 2007. . Retrieved January 11, 2009.

[110] "American Religious Identification Survey" (http://www.americanreligionsurvey-aris.org). Institute for the Study of Secularism in Society and Culture. 2008. . Retrieved April 21, 2008.

[111] Vegh, Steven G. (November 10, 2006). "2nd Georgia church joins moderate Va. Baptist association" (http://hamptonroads.com/node/180361). *The Virginian-Pilot*. . Retrieved December 18, 2007.

[112] "SBCV passes 500 mark" (http://www.bpnews.net/bpnews.asp?id=26884). Baptist Press. November 20, 2007. . Retrieved December 18, 2007.

[113] "U.S. Religion Map and Religious Populations" (http://religions.pewforum.org/pdf/report-religious-landscape-study-full.pdf) (PDF). The Pew Forum on Religion & Public Life. September 11, 2008. . Retrieved September 29, 2008.

[114] "State Membership Report (1990–2000 Change)" (http://www.thearda.com/mapsReports/reports/state/51_compare_Adherents.asp). Association of Religion Data Archives. 2000. . Retrieved September 29, 2008.

[115] "ARIS 2001: Key Findings" (http://www.gc.cuny.edu/Faculty/GC-Faculty-Activities/ARIS--American-Religious-Identification-Survey/Key-findings). The Graduate Center, The City University of New York. 2001. . Retrieved November 26, 2011.

[116] Boorstein, Michelle (November 14, 2007). "Trial Begins in Clash Over Va. Church Property" (http://www.washingtonpost.com/wp-dyn/content/article/2007/11/13/AR2007111302078.html). *The Washington Post*. . Retrieved November 19, 2007.

[117] "USA-Virginia" (http://beta-newsroom.lds.org/country/usa-virginia). *Country Profiles*. The Church of Jesus Christ of Latter-day Saints. 2010. . Retrieved November 14, 2010.

[118] Olitzky 1996, p. 359

[119] Alfaham, Sarah (September 11, 2008). "Muslims' visibility in region growing" (http://www.dailyprogress.com/cdp/news/state_regional/article/muslims_visibility_in_region_growing/27575/). *Richmond Times-Dispatch* (Charlottesville Daily Progress). . Retrieved May 2, 2009.

[120] "Megachurch Search Results" (http://hirr.hartsem.edu/cgi-bin/mega/db.pl?db=default&uid=default&view_records=1&ID=*&sb=3&so=descend). Hartford Institute for Religion Research. 2008. . Retrieved November 7, 2008.

[121] Vogel, Steve (May 27, 2007). "How the Pentagon Got Its Shape" (http://www.washingtonpost.com/wp-dyn/content/article/2007/05/23/AR2007052301296.html). *The Washington Post*. . Retrieved April 21, 2009.

[122] "The Virginia Department of Labor and Industry: Frequently Asked Questions: Labor & Employment Law" (http://www.doli.virginia.gov/laborlaw/laborlaw_faqs.html). . Retrieved November13,2011.

[123] "Virginia State Energy Profiles" (http://tonto.eia.doe.gov/state/state_energy_profiles.cfm?sid=VA). *Energy Information Administration*. United States Department of Energy. June 26, 2008. . Retrieved June 27, 2008.

[124] "Virginia facts" (http://travel.nationalgeographic.com/places/states/state_virginia.html). National Geographic. April 2, 2008. . Retrieved April 12, 2008.

[125] "Regional and State Employment and Unemployment Summary" (http://www.bls.gov/news.release/laus.nr0.htm). *Bureau of Labor Statistics*. March 26, 2010. . Retrieved March 26, 2010.

[126] "GDP by State" (http://greyhill.com/gdp-by-state). Greyhill Advisors. . Retrieved 16 September 2011.

[127] "Per capita personal income" (http://www.bea.gov/regional/reis/drill.cfm?table=CA1-3&catable=CA1-3&lc=30&years=2005&rformat=display&areatype=LOCAL&sort=1). *Regional Economic Information System*. Bureau of Economic Analysis. April 2007. . Retrieved November 24, 2007.

[128] Poersch, Gregory (April 2, 2008). "1 of Out of 11 Workers in Virginia in Tech Industry, Highest Concentration in the Nation, AeA Says" (http://www.reuters.com/article/pressRelease/idUS44925+02-Apr-2008+PRN20080402). *American Electronics Association*. Reuters. . Retrieved October 7, 2007.

[129] Garber, Kent (March 24, 2009). "The Internet's Hidden Energy Hogs: Data Servers" (http://www.usnews.com/news/energy/articles/2009/03/24/the-internets-hidden-energy-hogs-data-servers). *U.S. News & World Report*. . Retrieved April 12, 2011.

[130] Austin, Scott (August 4, 2010). "Interactive Map: The United States of Venture Capital" (http://blogs.wsj.com/venturecapital/2011/08/04/interactive-map-the-united-states-of-venture-capital/). *The Wall Street Journal*. . Retrieved August 6, 2010.

[131] Badenhausen, Kurt (September 23, 2009). "The Best States for Business" (http://www.forbes.com/2009/09/23/best-states-for-business-beltway-best-states.html). *Forbes*. . Retrieved March 27, 2010.

[132] Cohn, Scott (June 28, 2011). "Virginia named [[America's Top States For Business|America's Top State for Business (http://www.usatoday.com/money/companies/2011-06-28-cnbc-virginia-top-state_n.htm)] in 2011"]. *CNBC*. . Retrieved June 28, 2011.

[133] "20 Minn. companies make newest Fortune 500" (http://hosted.ap.org/dynamic/stories/M/MN_FORTUNE_500_MINNESOTA_MNOL-). *Rochester Post-Bulletin*. Associated Press. May 5, 2011. . Retrieved May 5, 2011.

[134] Helderman, Rosalind S. (May 6, 2010). "Virginia's love-hate relationship with federal spending" (http://www.washingtonpost.com/wp-dyn/content/article/2010/05/05/AR2010050505205.html). *The Washington Post*. . Retrieved May 26, 2010.

[135] Ellis, Nicole Anderson (September 1, 2008). "Virginia weighs its dependence on defense spending" (http://www.virginiabusiness.com/index.php/news/article/virginia-weighs-its-dependence-on-defense-spending/1829/). *Virginia Business*. . Retrieved May 26, 2010.

[136] "Virginia Finally Comes Into Play" (http://www.cbsnews.com/stories/2008/10/17/eveningnews/main4530304.shtml). CBS News. October 17, 2008. . Retrieved October 20, 2008.

[137] Fox, Justin (February 8, 2007). "The Federal Job Machine" (http://www.time.com/time/magazine/article/0,9171,1587284-2,00.html). *Time*. . Retrieved November 7, 2007.

[138] "Virginia Agriculture — Facts and Figures" (http://www.vdacs.virginia.gov/agfacts/index.shtml). Virginia Department of Agriculture and Consumer Services. 2009. . Retrieved October 6, 2009.

[139] McNatt, Linda (October 17, 2007). "Tomato moves into the top money-making spot in Virginia" (http://hamptonroads.com/node/354831). *The Virginian-Pilot*. . Retrieved October 18, 2007.

[140] "Virginia" (http://www.agcensus.usda.gov/Publications/2007/Online_Highlights/County_Profiles/Virginia/cp99051.pdf) (PDF). *2007 Census of Agriculture*. United States Census Bureau. July 17, 2009. . Retrieved October 6, 2009.

[141] "NOAA Working to Restore Oysters in the Chesapeake Bay" (http://www.magazine.noaa.gov/stories/mag165.htm). *National Oceanic and Atmospheric Administration*. March 31, 2005. . Retrieved February 14, 2008.

[142] "Assessment of the Profitability and Viability of Virginia Wineries" (http://www.vdacs.virginia.gov/pdffiles/vawinery.pdf) (PDF). *MKF Research LLC*. Virginia Department of Agriculture and Consumer Services. June 2007. . Retrieved June 26, 2008.

[143] "Sales and Use Tax" (http://www.tax.virginia.gov/site.cfm?alias=salesusetax#Retail). *Virginia Department of Taxation*. February 23, 2010. . Retrieved May 6, 2010.

[144] "Virginia Tax Facts" (http://www.tax.virginia.gov/Documents/Tax Facts - 7-1-2011.pdf) (PDF). Virginia Department of Taxation. July 1, 2011. . Retrieved November 26, 2011.

[145] Fischer & Kelly 2000, pp. 102–103

[146] McGraw 2005, p. 14

[147] "Roots of Virginia Culture" (http://www.folklife.si.edu/resources/2007Festival/VA_Signs/SFF07_VA_Intro_Map.pdf) (PDF). *Smithsonian Folklife Festival 2007*. Smithsonian Institution. July 5, 2007. . Retrieved September 29, 2008.

[148] Clay III, Edwin S.; Bangs, Patricia (May 9, 2005). "Virginia's Many Voices" (http://www.baconsrebellion.com/Issues05/05-09/Curious.htm). Fairfax County, Virginia. . Retrieved 2010-11-14.

[149] Miller, John J. (August 2, 2005). "Exotic Tangier" (http://article.nationalreview.com/?q=YjU1OTc0Y2ViOWQ1MjJmMTA5NTQ1ODJlZTUyNzY3MmI). *National Review*. . Retrieved October 9, 2008.

[150] Gray & Robinson 2004, pp. 81, 103

[151] Kirkpatrick, Mary Alice. "Summary of Jurgen: A Comedy of Justice" (http://docsouth.unc.edu/southlit/cabell1/summary.html). *Library of Southern Literature*. University of North Carolina. . Retrieved August 18, 2009.

[152] Lehmann-Haupt, Christopher (November 2, 2006). "William Styron, Novelist, Dies at 81" (http://www.nytimes.com/2006/11/02/books/02styron.html). *The New York Times*. . Retrieved August 18, 2009.

[153] Dirda, Michael (November 7, 2004). "A Coed in Full" (http://www.washingtonpost.com/wp-dyn/articles/A26738-2004Nov4.html). *The Washington Post*. . Retrieved October 3, 2009.

[154] Yancey, Dwayne (January 11, 2011). "McDonnell names a new poet laureate" (http://blogs.roanoke.com/politics/2011/01/14/mcdonnell-names-a-new-poet-laureate/). *The Roanoke Times*. . Retrieved January 22, 2011.

[155] Williamson 2008, p. 41

[156] Keller, Christian B. (2001). "Pennsylvania and Virginia Germans during the Civil War" (http://www.vahistorical.org/publications/Abstract_1091_Keller.htm). *Virginia Magazine of History and Biography* (Virginia Historical Society) **109**: 37–86. . Retrieved April 12, 2008.

[157] "State Arts Agency Funding and Grant Making" (http://www.nasaa-arts.org/Research/Grant-Making/2010_funding_and_grantmaking.pdf) (PDF) (Press release). National Assembly of State Arts Agencies. March 2010. . Retrieved May 3, 2010.

[158] Smith 2008, pp. 22–25

[159] Howard, Burnham & Burnham 2006, pp. 88, 206, 292

[160] "Mission & History" (http://www.virginia.edu/vfh/mission.html). *Virginia Foundation for the Humanities*. 2007. . Retrieved December 9, 2007.

[161] Scott & Scott 2004, pp. 307–308

[162] Howard, Burnham & Burnham 2006, pp. 165–166

[163] Goodwin 2008, p. 170

[164] Rice, Ruth (November 27, 2006). "Holiday magic: Arcadia play tells tale of Christmas poem" (http://tribune-democrat.com/events/x519134240/Holiday-magic-Arcadia-play-tells-tale-of-Christmas-poem). *The Tribune-Democrat*. . Retrieved July 7, 2010.

[165] Howard, Burnham & Burnham 2006, pp. 29, 121, 363, 432

[166] Goodwin 2008, pp. 23–25

[167] Meyer, Marianne (June 7, 2007). "Live!" (http://www.washingtonpost.com/wp-dyn/content/article/2007/06/06/AR2007060601032.html). *The Washington Post*. . Retrieved November 7, 2008.

[168] "Virginia Lake Festival" (http://www.virginia.org/site/description.asp?attrID=39216). Virginia Tourism Corporation. 2008. . Retrieved September 8, 2008.

[169] "Local Television Market Universe Estimates" (http://www.tvb.org/media/file/Nielsen_2010_2011_DMA_RANKS.pdf). September 25, 2010. . Retrieved May 6, 2011.

[170] "Virginia TV Stations" (http://www.mondotimes.com/world/usa/tv.html?state=46). MondoTimes. 2011. . Retrieved May 6, 2011.

[171] "FM Query" (http://www.fcc.gov/fcc-bin/fmq?state=VA). Federal Communications Commission. May 6, 2011. . Retrieved May 6, 2011.

[172] "AM Query" (http://www.fcc.gov/fcc-bin/amq?state=VA). Federal Communications Commission. May 6, 2011. . Retrieved May 6, 2011.

[173] "Highest Circulation Virginia Newspapers" (http://www.mondonewspapers.com/usa/circulation/virginia.html). *Mondo Newspapers*. September 30, 2010. . Retrieved May 1, 2011.

[174] "USA Today posts small circulation gain as it undergoes a revamp to counter Internet threat" (http://au.finance.yahoo.com/news/USA-Today-posts-small-apf-2688780192.html?x=0). *yahoo*. Associated Press. April 20, 2011. . Retrieved November 1, 2011.

[175] "Monticello and the University of Virginia in Charlottesville" (http://whc.unesco.org/en/list/442). UNESCO. October 15, 2008. . Retrieved October 14, 2008.

[176] "State Education Data Profiles" (http://nces.ed.gov/programs/stateprofiles/sresult.asp?mode=full&displaycat=7&s1=51). National Assessment of Educational Progress. 2005. . Retrieved December 25, 2007.

[177] "Quality Counts 2011" (http://www.edweek.org/media/ew/qc/2011/QualityCounts2011_PressRelease.pdf) (PDF). *Education Week*. January 11, 2011. . Retrieved May 5, 2011.

[178] "Virginia School Report Card" (http://www.doe.virginia.gov/VDOE/src/index.shtml). Virginia Department of Education. 2007. . Retrieved February 2, 2008.

[179] Sieff, Kevin (October 1, 2010). "Virginia high school graduation rate increases" (http://www.washingtonpost.com/wp-dyn/content/article/2010/09/30/AR2010093007174.html). *The Washington Post*. . Retrieved May 6, 2011.

[180] Will, George F. (June 6, 2010). "Why should education be exempt from recession budgeting?" (http://www.washingtonpost.com/wp-dyn/content/article/2010/06/04/AR2010060403753.html). *The Washington Post*. . Retrieved May 10, 2011.

[181] "State Report Cards" (https://p1pe.doe.virginia.gov/reportcard/report.do?division=All&schoolName=All) (PDF). *Virginia Department of Education*. April 28, 2011. . Retrieved May 1, 2011.

[182] "Virginia Public Schools — By Division" (http://doe.virginiainteractive.org/vdoe_directories/PublicSchoolsByDivisions.aspx). Virginia Department of Education. 2010. . Retrieved April 6, 2010.

[183] "Governor's School Program" (http://www.doe.virginia.gov/instruction/governors_school_programs/index.shtml). Virginia Department of Education. 2010. . Retrieved February 12, 2010.

[184] "State Recognized Accredited Schools" (http://www.vcpe.org/2011-02-20 VCPE Accredited.pdf) (PDF). Virginia Council for Private Education. February 20, 2011. . Retrieved May 6, 2011.

[185] "Non-Accredited Schools" (http://www.vcpe.org/2011-03-08 VCPE Non-Accredited.pdf) (PDF). Virginia Council for Private Education. March 8, 2011. . Retrieved May 6, 2011.

[186] "Home-Schooled Students and Religious Exemptions" (http://www.doe.virginia.gov/statistics_reports/enrollment/home_school_religious_exempt/2010_2011.xls) (XLS). Virginia Department of Education. December 16, 2010. . Retrieved May 5, 2011.

[187] "College Navigator — Search Results" (http://nces.ed.gov/collegenavigator/?s=VA). *National Center for Education Statistics*. United States Department of Education. 2011. . Retrieved May 1, 2011.

[188] "Top Public National Universities 2010" (http://colleges.usnews.rankingsandreviews.com/best-colleges/national-top-public). *U.S. News and World Report*. April 15, 2010. . Retrieved July 6, 2010.

[189] "History & Traditions" (http://www.wm.edu/about/history/). College of William and Mary. 2008. . Retrieved October 22, 2008.

[190] "Rankings — Fine Arts — Graduate Schools" (http://grad-schools.usnews.rankingsandreviews.com/best-graduate-schools/top-fine-arts-schools/rankings). *U.S. News and World Report*. April 15, 2010. . Retrieved July 2, 2010.

[191] "JMU Holds Top Public Regional Rank for 14th Year in 'U.S. News' Survey" (http://web.archive.org/web/20070830075957/http://www.jmu.edu/jmuweb/general/news/general8824.shtml). *Public Affairs* (James Madison University). August 17, 2007. Archived from the original (http://www.jmu.edu/jmuweb/general/news/general8824.shtml) on 2007-08-30. . Retrieved April 11, 2008.

[192] Conley, Jay (August 12, 2007). "'Just like the guys': A decade of women at VMI" (http://www.roanoke.com/news/roanoke/wb/127669). *The Roanoke Times*. . Retrieved October 22, 2008.

[193] Conley, Jay (August 22, 2008). "HVMI retains U.S. News' rank as No. 3" (http://www.roanoke.com/news/roanoke/wb/174003). *The Roanoke Times*. . Retrieved September 30, 2008.

[194] "In head count, George Mason edges VCU" (http://www2.timesdispatch.com/rtd/news/local/education/article/GMUU15_20091014-221605/299431/). Richmond Times-Disbatch. 2009. . Retrieved July 1, 2009.

[195] "Fast Facts" (http://www.vccs.edu/WhoWeAre/FastFacts/tabid/79/Default.aspx). Virginia's Community Colleges. 2008. . Retrieved August 3, 2009.

[196] "Virginia" (http://www.americashealthrankings.org/yearcompare/2009/2010/VA.aspx). *America's Health Rankings 2009*. United Health Foundation. November 9, 2009. . Retrieved May 6, 2011.

[197] Kumar, Anita (August 4, 2009). "Infant Mortality in Virginia Falls to All-Time Low" (http://www.washingtonpost.com/wp-dyn/content/article/2009/08/04/AR2009080401672.html). *The Washington Post*. . Retrieved August 4, 2009.

[198] "Virginia – 2009 Overweight and Obesity (BMI)" (http://apps.nccd.cdc.gov/BRFSS/display.asp?cat=OB&yr=2009&qkey=4409&state=VA). Centers for Disease Control and Prevention. 2010. . Retrieved May 6, 2011.

[199] "Virginia – 2007 Exercise" (http://apps.nccd.cdc.gov/BRFSS/display.asp?cat=EX&yr=2009&qkey=4347&state=VA). Centers for Disease Control and Prevention. 2010. . Retrieved May 6, 2011.

[200] "Measuring Virginia's Obesity Rates" (http://www.vaperforms.virginia.gov/indicators/healthFamily/obesity.php). Virginia Performs. 2009. . Retrieved March 25, 2009.

[201] "Va. restaurant owners bracing for smoke ban" (http://www.washingtontimes.com/news/2009/nov/30/restaurant-owners-to-brace-for-smoke-ban). *The Washington Times*. Associated Press. November 30, 2009. . Retrieved May 6, 2011.

[202] "Hospital Compare" (http://www.hospitalcompare.hhs.gov/hospital-results.aspx?state=VA&htype=0&stype=GENERAL&). United States Department of Health and Human Services. December 11, 2010. . Retrieved April 12, 2011.

[203] "University of Virginia Medical Center, Charlottesville" (http://www.usnews.com/listings/hospitals/6344000). *Best Hospitals*. U.S. News & World Report. 2007. . Retrieved February 6, 2008.

[204] "Sentara Norfolk General Hospital-Sentara Heart Hospital, Norfolk, Va." (http://www.usnews.com/listings/hospitals/6340620). *Best Hospitals*. U.S. News & World Report. 2007. . Retrieved February 6, 2008.

[205] Szabo, Liz (May 12, 2004). "America's first 'test-tube baby'" (http://www.usatoday.com/news/health/2004-05-12-testtube-baby-usat_x.htm). *USA Today*. . Retrieved February 6, 2008.

[206] Walker, Keith (December 9, 2008). "Va. gets high disaster preparedness marks" (http://www.insidenova.com/isn/news/local/article/va._gets_high_disaster_preparedness_marks/25973/). Inside NoVA. . Retrieved December 10, 2008.

[207] O'Leary, Amy A. (April 1998). "Beyond the Byrd Road Act: VDOT's Relationship with Virginia's Urban Counties" (http://www.virginiadot.org/vtrc/main/online_reports/pdf/98-r29.pdf) (PDF). *Virginia Department of Transportation*. . Retrieved October 3, 2009.

[208] "Virginia's Highway System" (http://www.virginiadot.org/about/vdot_hgwy_sys.asp). Virginia Department of Transportation. January 12, 2011. . Retrieved May 1, 2011.

[209] Mummolo, Jonathan (September 19, 2007). "A Ranking Writ In Brake Lights: D.C. 2nd in Traffic" (http://www.washingtonpost.com/wp-dyn/content/article/2007/09/18/AR2007091800777.html). *The Washington Post*. . Retrieved March 29, 2008.

[210] "Measuring Traffic Congestion in Virginia" (http://vaperforms.virginia.gov/indicators/transportation/trafficCongestion.php). Virginia Performs. April 9, 2009. . Retrieved April 30, 2009.

[211] Buske, Jennifer (October 14, 2010). "VRE sets ridership record" (http://voices.washingtonpost.com/dr-gridlock/2010/10/vre_sets_ridership_record.html). *The Washington Post*. . Retrieved April 12, 2011.

[212] Hosh, Kafia A. (April 15, 2011). "Federal, Va. officials object to underground Metro station at Dulles airport" (http://www.washingtonpost.com/local/federal-va-officials-object-to-underground-metro-station-at-dulles-airport/2011/04/13/AF6SK7kD_story.html). *The Washington Post*. . Retrieved May 6, 2011.

[213] "Ferry Information" (http://www.virginiadot.org/travel/ferry.asp). Virginia Department of Transportation. December 4, 2007. . Retrieved February 14, 2008.

[214] "Airports" (http://www.doav.virginia.gov/airports.htm). Virginia Department of Aviation. 2006. . Retrieved April 12, 2008.

[215] "Port/Maritime" (http://hamptonroadsperforms.org/indicators/economy/ports.php). Virginia Performs. 2009. . Retrieved May 2, 2009.

[216] Goodwin 2008, p. 319

[217] Ruane, Michael E. (December 17, 2006). "At Va. Spaceport, Rocket Launches 1,000 Dreams" (http://www.washingtonpost.com/wp-dyn/content/article/2006/12/16/AR2006121600880.html). *The Washington Post*. . Retrieved September 10, 2009.

[218] Hart, Kim (April 21, 2007). "Travel agency launches tourists on out-of-this-world adventures" (http://seattletimes.nwsource.com/html/businesstechnology/2003675354_spacetours21.html?syndication=rss). *The Seattle Times*. . Retrieved May 26, 2008.

[219] Helderman, Rosalind S.; Jenkins, Chris L. (May 7, 2006). "Latest Budget Standoff Met With Shrugs" (http://www.washingtonpost.com/wp-dyn/content/article/2006/05/06/AR2006050601099_pf.html). *The Washington Post*. . Retrieved November 24, 2007.

[220] Strum, Albert L. (June 1977). "Commentaries on the Constitution of Virginia by A. E. Dick Howard". *The American Political Science Review* **71** (2): 714–715. JSTOR 1978427.

[221] "Virginia Courts In Brief" (http://www.courts.state.va.us/courts/cib.pdf) (PDF). Virginia Judicial System. May 5, 2009. . Retrieved August 17, 2009.

[222] Lettner, Kimberly. "Message from the Chief" (http://www.vcp.state.va.us/message.htm). The Division of Capitol Police. . Retrieved September 10, 2009.

[223] Listman, Jr., John W.; Carter, III, Lt. Col. Chester C. (August 20, 2007). "Serving Commonwealth and Country" (http://vko.va.ngb.army.mil/VirginiaGuard/history/overview.html). Virginia Army National Guard. . Retrieved February 11, 2008.

[224] Williams, Carol J. (September 23, 2010). "Virginia's execution of a woman may signal shift in national thinking" (http://www.latimes.com/news/local/la-me-condemned-women-20100924,0,1991421.story). *Los Angeles Times*. . Retrieved September 24, 2010.

[225] "Quick Facts for Virginia" (http://www.washingtonpost.com/ac2/wp-dyn/local-explorer/quick-facts?search=VA). *LocalExplorer* (Washington Post). 2009. . Retrieved September 11, 2009.

[226] Rosenwald, Michael S. (April 13, 2011). *The Washington Post*. Va. returning prisoners to jail at lower-than-average rate, study shows. Retrieved April 13, 2011.

[227] Sweeney, James R. (1999). ""Sheep without a Shepherd": The New Deal Faction in the Virginia Democratic Party" (http://www.questia.com/googleScholar.qst?docId=5001263885). *Presidential Studies Quarterly* **29** (2): 438. doi:10.1111/1741-5705.00043. . Retrieved March 31, 2008.

[228] Burchett, Michael H. (Summer 1997). "Promise and prejudice: Wise County, Virginia and the Great Migration, 1910–1920". *The Journal of Negro History* **82** (3): 312–327. doi:10.2307/2717675. JSTOR 2717675.

[229] Eisman, Dale (October 25, 2006). "Webb, Allen court Hispanic, white-collar voters in N. Va." (http://hamptonroads.com/node/172411). *The Virginian-Pilot*. . Retrieved March 29, 2008.

[230] Turque, Bill; Wiggins, Ovetta; Stewart, Nikita (February 13, 2008). "In Virginia, Results Signal A State in Play for November" (http://www.washingtonpost.com/wp-dyn/content/article/2008/02/12/AR2008021203200_pf.html). *The Washington Post*. . Retrieved

September 29, 2008.

[231] Miller, Gary; Schofield, Norman (May 2003). "Activists and Partisan Realignment in the United States". *The American Political Science Review* **97** (2): 245–260. JSTOR 3118207.

[232] Craig, Tim (December 11, 2007). "Tensions Could Hurt Majority in Va. Senate" (http://www.washingtonpost.com/wp-dyn/content/story/2007/12/10/ST2007121001571.html). *The Washington Post*. . Retrieved December 23, 2007.

[233] Clemons, Michael L.; Jones, Charles E. (July 2000). "African American Legislative Politics in Virginia". *Journal of Black Studies* **30** (6, Special Issue: African American State Legislative Politics): 744–767. doi:10.1177/002193470003000603. JSTOR 2645922.

[234] Craig, Tim; Kumar, Anita (November 8, 2007). "Kaine Hails 'Balance' in New Political Landscape" (http://www.washingtonpost.com/wp-dyn/content/article/2007/11/07/AR2007110700553_2.html). *The Washington Post*. . Retrieved November 7, 2007.

[235] Helderman, Rosalind S.; Kumar, Anita (November 4, 2009). "GOP reclaims Virginia" (http://www.washingtonpost.com/wp-dyn/content/article/2009/11/03/AR2009110300371.html). *The Washington Post*. . Retrieved November 4, 2009.

[236] Lewis, Bob (November 10, 2011). "GOP claims Va. Senate majority after Dem concedes" (http://www.boston.com/news/nation/washington/articles/2011/11/10/gop_claims_va_senate_majority_after_dem_concedes/). *The Boston Globe*. Associated Press. . Retrieved November 15, 2011.

[237] Murray, Mark (April 16, 2009). "Shad Planking kicks Virginia race into gear" (http://www.msnbc.msn.com/id/30248457/). MSNBC. . Retrieved May 7, 2009.

[238] Page, Susan (November 26, 2006). "Election '06: Lessons learned by dissecting votes" (http://www.usatoday.com/news/washington/2006-11-26-election-lessons_x.htm). *USA Today*. . Retrieved December 12, 2007.

[239] Kumar, Anita (November 5, 2008). "Warner Rolls Past His Fellow Former Governor" (http://www.washingtonpost.com/wp-dyn/content/article/2008/11/04/AR2008110404091.html). *The Washington Post*. . Retrieved November 5, 2008.

[240] Lewis, Bob (November 5, 2008). "Obama first Democrat to take Virginia in 44 years" (http://www.foxnews.com/wires/2008Nov05/0,4670,ElectionVirginia,00.html). Associated Press. Fox News. . Retrieved January 9, 2009.

[241] Wood, Norm (December 28, 2008). "Bowl streak began humbly" (http://www.dailypress.com/sports/dp-spt_techbowlstreak_1228dec28,0,2384850.story). *Daily Press*. . Retrieved September 11, 2009.

[242] Minium, Harry (July 19, 2001). "Region Works to Attract Franchise Area Makes "Short List" for Existing Team's Move" (http://web.archive.org/web/20080226215152/http://www.facilityplanners.com/news/pdf/Professional+Sports+in+Hampton+Roads.pdf) (PDF). *The Virginian-Pilot*. Archived from the original (http://www.facilityplanners.com/news/pdf/Professional Sports in Hampton Roads.pdf) on 2008-02-26. . Retrieved December 9, 2007.

[243] Utt, Ronald D. (October 2, 1998). "Cities in Denial: The False Promise of Subsidized Tourist and Entertainment Complexes" (http://www.heritage.org/research/urbanissues/bg1223.cfm). *The Heritage Foundation*. . Retrieved October 3, 2009.

[244] Robinson, Tom (October 22, 2011). "Virginia Destroyers capture UFL title in 17-3 victory" (http://hamptonroads.com/2011/10/virginia-destroyers-capture-ufl-title-173-victory). *The Virginian-Pilot*. . Retrieved November 15, 2011.

[245] Fernandes, Deirdre (January 4, 2008). "Beach officials hope to lure Redskins' training camp to Sportsplex" (http://hamptonroads.com/2008/01/beach-officials-hope-lure-redskinsâ-training-camp-sportsplex). *The Virginian-Pilot*. . Retrieved April 12, 2008.

[246] "NASCAR in Virginia" (http://www.virginia.org/nascar/). *Virginia is for Lovers*. 2011. . Retrieved November 26, 2011.

[247] "Find MASN on your TV" (http://masnsports.com/2007/09/find-masn.html). *Mid-Atlantic Sports Network*. September 7, 2007. . Retrieved December 11, 2007.

[248] Borawski, Brian (September 27, 2006). "Business of Baseball Report" (http://www.hardballtimes.com/main/article/business-of-baseball-report120/). The Orioles Warehouse. . Retrieved April 12, 2008.

[249] O'Connor, John (April 2, 2010). "Squirrels will nest at Diamond for several years" (http://www2.timesdispatch.com/rtd/sports/minors/minors_baseball/article/BASE02_20100401-221608/334637/). *Richmond Times-Dispatch*. . Retrieved April 27, 2010.

[250] "Baseball in Virginia" (http://www.virginia.org/baseball/). Virginia is for Lovers. 2011. . Retrieved November 26, 2011.

[251] Sylwester, MaryJo; Witosky, Tom (February 18, 2004). "Athletic spending grows as academic funds dry up" (http://www.usatoday.com/sports/college/2004-02-18-athletic-spending-cover_x.htm). *USA Today*. . Retrieved August 16, 2010.

[252] Brady, Erik (December 14, 2006). "Virginia town is big game central" (http://www.usatoday.com/sports/college/football/2006-12-13-focus-salem_x.htm). *USA Today*. . Retrieved February 6, 2008.

[253] "Capitol Classroom" (http://legis.state.va.us/1_cap_class/9-12/9_12_emb_symb.html). Virginia General Assembly. December 13, 2007. . Retrieved April 12, 2008.

[254] Berrier, Ralph (January 11, 2008). "Carry me back to the state song search" (http://www.roanoke.com/columnists/berrier/wb/146590). *The Roanoke Times*. . Retrieved September 10, 2009.

[255] Sluss, Michael (March 2, 2006). "Proposed state song doesn't bring down the House" (http://www.roanoke.com/news/roanoke/wb/wb/xp-54991). *The Roanoke Times*. . Retrieved October 14, 2008.

Bibliography

- Abrams, Ann Uhry (1999). *The pilgrims and Pocahontas: rival myths of American origin* (http://books.google.com/?id=y4-ljMLfwp4C&pg=PR15). Boulder, CO: Westview Press. ISBN 0-8133-3497-7.
- Accordino, John J. (2000). *Captives of the Cold War Economy* (http://books.google.com/?id=S6TuEMY2clQC). Westport, CT: Greenwood Publishing Group. ISBN 0-2759-6561-9.
- Anderson, Fred (2000). *Crucible of War: The Seven Years' War and the Fate of Empire in British North America, 1754-1766* (http://books.google.com/books?id=-vMxLslZopgC). New York: Random House. ISBN 0375406425.
- Burnham, Bill; Burnham, Mary (2004). *Hiking Virginia: A Guide to Virginia's Greatest Hiking Adventures* (http://books.google.com/?id=VkKEooYDuToC). Guilford, CT: Globe Pequot. ISBN 0-7627-2747-0.
- Carroll, Steven; Miller, Mark (2002). *Wild Virginia: A Guide to Thirty Roadless Recreation Areas Including Shenandoah National Park* (http://books.google.com/?id=ymATg0mq8jkC). Guilford, CT: Globe Pequot. ISBN 0-7627-2315-7.
- Chambers, Douglas B. (2005). *Murder at Montpelier: Igbo Africans in Virginia* (http://books.google.com/?id=vqpoxEl_0_4C&pg=PA10). Jackson: University Press of Mississippi. ISBN 1-5780-6706-5.
- Conlin, Joseph R. (2009). *The American Past: A Survey of American History* (http://books.google.com/?id=tT2AEMiUXvwC&pg=PT57). Belmont, CA: Thomson Learning. ISBN 0-4955-6609-8.
- Cooper, Jean L. (2007). *A Guide to Historic Charlottesville and Albemarle County, Virginia* (http://books.google.com/?id=nCn4XrP_u0MC). Charleston, SC: The History Press. ISBN 1-596-29173-7.
- Dailey, Jane Elizabeth; Gilmore, Glenda Elizabeth; Simon, Bryant (2000). *Jumpin' Jim Crow: Southern Politics from Civil War to Civil Rights* (http://books.google.com/?id=yFvjsEYP7hAC&pg=PA90). Princeton, NJ: Princeton University Press. ISBN 0-6910-0193-6.
- Davis, David Brion (2006). *Inhuman Bondage: The Rise and Fall of Slavery in the New World*. New York: Oxford University Press. ISBN 0-1951-4073-7.
- *The Encyclopedia of Virginia*. **1** (4 ed.). St. Clair Shores, MI: Somerset Publishers. 1999. ISBN 0-4030-9753-3.
- Grizzard, Frank E.; Smith, D. Boyd (2007). *Jamestown Colony: a political, social, and cultural history* (http://books.google.com/books?id=555CzPsGLDMC&pg=PA128). Santa Barbara, CA: ABC-CLIO. ISBN 1-85109-637-X.
- Fischer, David Hackett; Kelly, James C. (2000). *Bound Away: Virginia and the Westward Movement*. Charlottesville: University of Virginia Press. ISBN 0-8139-1774-3.
- Goodwin, Bill (2008). *Frommer's Virginia* (http://books.google.com/?id=fnT2tRbE1vMC). Hoboken, NJ: John Wiley & Sons. ISBN 0-4701-7591-5.
- Gordon, John Steele (2004). *An Empire of Wealth: The Epic History of American Economic Power* (http://books.google.com/?id=rmsUs_KDgHAC&pg=PA17). New York: HarperCollins. ISBN 0-0600-9362-5.
- Gray, Richard J.; Robinson, Owen (2004). *A Companion to the Literature and Culture of the American South* (http://books.google.com/?id=v10uoRwUsuEC). Oxford: Wiley-Blackwell. ISBN 0-6312-2404-1.
- Gutzman, Kevin R. C. (2007). *Virginia's American Revolution: From Dominion to Republic, 1776–1840*. Lanham, MD: Lexington Books. ISBN 0-7391-2131-6.
- Hashaw, Tim (2007). *The Birth of Black America*. New York: Carroll & Graf Publishers. ISBN 0-7867-1718-1.
- Heinemann, Ronald L.; Kolp, John G.; Parent, Jr., Anthony S.; Shade, William G. (2007). *Old Dominion, New Commonwealth*. Charlottesville: University of Virginia Press. ISBN 0-8139-2609-2.
- Hoffer, Peter Charles (2006). *The Brave New World: A History of Early America*. Baltimore: JHU Press. ISBN 0-8018-8483-7.
- Howard, Blair; Burnham, Mary; Burnham, Bill (2006). *The Virginia Handbook* (http://books.google.com/?id=bX0t5dMokXYC) (3 ed.). Edison, NJ: Hunter Publishing. ISBN 1-5884-3512-1.
- Hubbard, Jr., Bill (2009). *American Boundaries: The Nation, the States, the Rectangular Survey* (http://books.google.com/?id=LMacwod5KLwC&pg=PA140). Chicago: University of Chicago Press. ISBN 0-2263-5591-8.

- Joseph, John Earl (2006). *Language and Politics* (http://books.google.com/?id=pJu5veUAo7kC&pg=PA63). Edinburgh: Edinburgh University Press. ISBN 0-7486-2453-8.
- McGraw, Eliza (June 24, 2005). *Two Covenants: Representations of Southern Jewishness* (http://books.google.com/?id=EzR13rJBwc4C&pg=PA14). Baton Rouge: Louisiana State University Press. ISBN 0-8071-3043-5.
- Miller, Kerby A.; Schrier, Arnold; Boling, Bruce D.; Doyle, David N. (2003). *Irish immigrants in the land of Canaan* (http://books.google.com/?id=bq79_YZ8ViIC). New York: Oxford University Press. ISBN 0-1950-4513-0.
- Moran, Michael G. (2007). *Inventing Virginia: Sir Walter Raleigh and the Rhetoric of Colonization, 1584–1590.* New York: Peter Lang. ISBN 0-8204-8694-9.
- Morgan, Lynda (1992). *Emancipation in Virginia's Tobacco Belt, 1850–1870.* Athens, GA: University of Georgia Press. ISBN 0-8203-1415-3.
- Morgan, Philip D. (1998). *Slave Counterpoint.* Chapel Hill: University of North Carolina Press. ISBN 0-8078-4717-8.
- Palmer, Tim (1998). *America by Rivers* (http://books.google.com/?id=ctA1eNFvI-oC&pg=PA49). Washington, D.C.: Island Press. ISBN 1-5596-3264-X.
- Pazzaglia, Frank James (2006). *Excursions in Geology and History: Field Trips in the Middle Atlantic States* (http://books.google.com/?id=vQdHRNitfOoC&pg=PA135). Boulder, CO: Geological Society of America. ISBN 0-8137-0008-6.
- Pinn, Anthony B. (2009). *African American Religious Cultures* (http://books.google.com/?id=xEEIY4Q1ZAIC&pg=PA175). Santa Barbara, CA: ABC-CLIO. ISBN 1-5760-7470-6.
- Olitzky, Kerry (1996). *The American Synagogue: A Historical Dictionary and Sourcebook.* Westport, CT: Greenwood Press. ISBN 0-3132-8856-9.
- Scott, David L.; Scott, Kay W. (2004). *Guide to the National Park Areas* (http://books.google.com/?id=Z8DCRmgPOewC&pg=PA307). Guilford, CT: Globe Pequot. ISBN 0-7627-2988-0.
- Smith, Julian (2008). *Moon Virginia: Including Washington, D.C.* (http://books.google.com/?id=WNEYCRIIQy4C&pg=PA152) (4 ed.). Berkeley, CA: Avalon Travel. ISBN 1-5988-0011-6.
- Robertson, James I. (1993). *Civil War Virginia: Battleground for a Nation* (http://books.google.com/?id=RKDkDZ6GLPcC). Charlottesville: University of Virginia Press. ISBN 0-8139-1457-4.
- Stewart, George (2008). *Names on the Land: A Historical Account of Place-Naming in the United States.* New York: Random House. ISBN 1-5901-7273-6.
- Vollmann, William T. (2002). *Argall: The True Story of Pocahontas and Captain John Smith* (http://books.google.com/?id=hh0WYbclptAC&pg=PA695). New York: Penguin Group. ISBN 0-1420-0150-3.
- Wallenstein, Peter (2007). *Cradle of America: Four Centuries of Virginia History* (http://books.google.com/?id=qiwSAAAAYAAJ). Lawrence, KS: University Press of Kansas. ISBN 978-0-7006-1507-0.
- Williamson, CiCi (2008). *The Best of Virginia Farms Cookbook and Tour Book* (http://books.google.com/?id=pnuFW6zT0T8C&pg=PA41). Birmingham, AL: Menasha Ridge Press. ISBN 0-8973-2657-1.

External links

General

- Virginia (http://www.dmoz.org/Regional/North_America/United_States/Virginia/) at the Open Directory Project
- Encyclopedia Virginia (http://encyclopediavirginia.org/about)

Government

- State Government website (http://portal.virginia.gov/)
- Virginia General Assembly (http://legis.state.va.us/)
- Virginia's Judicial system (http://www.courts.state.va.us/)

- Constitution of Virginia (http://legis.state.va.us/Laws/search/Constitution.htm)
- Virginia State and County Government Websites (http://www.virginia.n2genealogy.com/#government)

Tourism and recreation

- Virginia Tourism Website (http://www.virginia.org/)
- Virginia State Parks (http://www.dcr.virginia.gov/state_parks/state_park.shtml)
- Virginia Main Street Communities Travel (http://www.nps.gov/history/nr/travel/VAmainstreet/)
- WikiTravel guide (http://wikitravel.org/en/Virginia)

Culture and history

- Virginia Historical Society (http://www.vahistorical.org/)
- Virginia's First People (http://virginiaindians.pwnet.org/index.php)
- WPA Guide to the Old Dominion (http://xroads.virginia.edu/~HYPER/VAGuide/frame.html)
- Library of Virginia (http://www.lva.virginia.gov/)

Maps and Demographics

- USGS geographic resources of Virginia (http://www.usgs.gov/state/state.asp?State=VA)
- Virginia State Climatology Office (http://climate.virginia.edu/)
- Virginia State Fact Sheet (http://www.ers.usda.gov/statefacts/va.htm)

Related information

gag:Virginia mrj:Виргини

Article Sources and Contributors

Senior_status *Source*: http://en.wikipedia.org/w/index.php?title=Senior_status *Contributors*: Anonymous Dissident, BD2412, Corixidae, DLJessup, ERcheck, Eastlaw, FoekeNoppert, Henrygb, Lockesdonkey, N2e, Neutrality, Newyorkbrad, PaulHanson, Rich Farmbrough, Richard75, Rillian, Rrius, Simon Dodd, That Guy, From That Show!, Tom, 10 anonymous edits

United_States_federal_judge *Source*: http://en.wikipedia.org/w/index.php?title=United_States_federal_judge *Contributors*: Arthur Rubin, Axios023, BD2412, Bathosrex, Bazj, Betacommand, Blanchardb, BoBo, Captiantwig, Chaoshexa, ChrisCork, Coolcaesar, Csari, Dannyc77, Decltype, Dreamrabbit, Elendil's Heir, Ellsworth, Epbr123, Epolk, Famspear, Farolif, JHunterJ, JJJJust, JPMcGrath, Jarvishunt, Jigen III, Jusdafax, Kay Sieverding, Kvdveer, Lethe, LittleOldMe, Lotje, Materialscientist, Memethvin, Michael Hardy, Neutrality, Newprogressive, NoSeptember, Pacotaco9, PaulHanson, Postdlf, Qq19342174, Rekleov, Sarkar112, Savidan, SchruteFarms, Snigbrook, Syrthiss, TCY, Tapom, The Rationalist, The Thing That Should Not Be, Tide rolls, Vishnava, Wuzzy, 54 anonymous edits

United_States_federal_courts *Source*: http://en.wikipedia.org/w/index.php?title=United_States_federal_courts *Contributors*: Ajdz, Andeggs, BD2412, Bejnar, Blanchardb, Bobmack89x, Bobo192, BoredTerry, Boundlessly, BradPatrick, CapitalR, Cflm001, Chart123, Cherubino, Chrism, Coolcaesar, Cquan, Davepape, Davidkinnen, Dnuffer, Dreamrabbit, Eastlaw, Epolk, Esrever, Evil Monkey, Excirial, Famspear, Flyguy33, Gilliam, GoldRingChip, Hubertfarnsworth, Innab, Int21h, ItsZippy, Jamesontai, Jdlund, Johnokray, Kumioko, Lindsay123, Lotje, McSly, MeDrake, Michael Hardy, Mild Bill Hiccup, Mklbtz, Neuroscientist, Neutrality, Newyorkbrad, NuclearWarfare, Nuttycoconut, Patchouli, R'n'B, Rich Farmbrough, RussBlau, Sardanaphalus, Seddon, Sirex98, Srich32977, Steamclock, Sylent, THEN WHO WAS PHONE?, Taupe, Toytoy, Unioneagle, User27091, Wavelength, Welsh, Zonkman, 110 anonymous edits

Law_clerk *Source*: http://en.wikipedia.org/w/index.php?title=Law_clerk *Contributors*: AFethke, Apokrif, BD2412, Baronnet, Bbb23, Bdpark, Bender235, BetaCentauri, BoBo, Boratborat, Brian Brockmeyer, Bwrs, Chensiyuan, Chicheley, Choalbaton, Clerko99999, Coolcaesar, D6, Dale Arnett, DethmeOw, Druben01, DynamoDegsy, Eastlaw, Edcolins, EdgarMCMLXXXI, Eric-Wester, Eric80hi, Flibjib8, Fluffernutter, Fmhmoreira, FosseTheCat, FrankTobia, Fred Bauder, Gaius Cornelius, Galaxiaad, Gator1, Geeoharee, Gettingtoit, GlassCobra, Harro5, Hebbgd, Hu12, Iridescent, J-Zeth, JamesReyes, Jaycee50, Jjh2003, John Cardinal, LaszloWalrus, Lincolnite, Lionelleo, MementoVivere, MrB, Mterrell85, Mytildebang, Neutrality, NoSeptember, OCNative, Oswald22, Ozoneliar, PRRfan, Peyna, Piano non troppo, Pmaccabe, Portillo, PullUpYourSocks, Reticulatory, Rjwilmsi, Rlove, Ryeh123, Schutz, Scwlong, Shinerunner, Shoora0071, SimonP, Skittleys, Texture, Thus Blogged Anderson, Tolrosebud, Tomas e, Zenohockey, 268 anonymous edits

United_States_Court_of_International_Trade *Source*: http://en.wikipedia.org/w/index.php?title=United_States_Court_of_International_Trade *Contributors*: 1337h4xx0rs, Abstract Idiot, Adam sk, Americasroof, Americus55, Apple1976, BD2412, Bjoel5785, BjoernZ, Eastlaw, Epolk, Fram, GoldRingChip, Grutness, ILaw, JamesMLane, PatrickFlaherty, PaulHanson, PullUpYourSocks, Pvmoutside, RFD, RussBlau, Safiel, Station1, Tim!, Toytoy, 17 anonymous edits

John_Wesley_Warrington *Source*: http://en.wikipedia.org/w/index.php?title=John_Wesley_Warrington *Contributors*: 8th Ohio Volunteers, BD2412, Reedy, Roseohioresident, Samiam4, Spacini

Supreme_Court_of_Virginia *Source*: http://en.wikipedia.org/w/index.php?title=Supreme_Court_of_Virginia *Contributors*: Alansohn, BD2412, Benuski, CommonsDelinker, FoekeNoppert, GreatWhiteNortherner, Ikip, JHunterJ, Jarvishunt, Kubigula, Lcarscad, LilHelpa, Lincolnite, Marcinjeske, Martin451, Morgan Riley, Muzi, Postdlf, PullUpYourSocks, Rad Racer, Rbraunwa, Rfc1394, Rpogge, Sardanaphalus, TJRC, Taco325i, The Founders Intent, TidewaterLawyer, Todowd, TonyTheTiger, VASupCtHist, VirginiaLaw, Wiki9lexus, Woohookitty, 57 anonymous edits

Iowa_Court_of_Appeals *Source*: http://en.wikipedia.org/w/index.php?title=Iowa_Court_of_Appeals *Contributors*: BD2412, Ctjf83, Eastlaw, Ilamb94, Johnjonesjr, Philosopher, 4 anonymous edits

Virginia *Source*: http://en.wikipedia.org/w/index.php?title=Virginia *Contributors*: 0, 0x6D667061, 105683EEE, 11abeeston, 123456llama, 14dpop, 15qdotnet, 4twenty42o, 525252a, A mirror, A1%, A2Kafir, AVand, AaronCBurke, Abductive, Abeg92, Abh9h, Abrech, Absolutevodka, Acroterion, Adams1311, Addihockey10, Addison0426, AdjustShift, Admiral Norton, Ahassan05, Ahoerstemeier, Aitias, Aivazovsky, Ajani57, AjaxSmack, Ajm1205, Al Silonov, Alansohn, AlbertHerring, Albyva, Alcarcalimo2364, Alex1011, AlexanderWinston, AlexiusHoratius, Alexwcovington, Allstar86, Allstarecho, AlphaPyro, Amatulic, Amazonien, Amish 01, Amyandile, Andre Engels, AndrewHowse, Andrwsc, Andy Marchbanks, Andy120290, Andycjp, Angielaj, Angr, Angrysockhop, Animum, AnnaFrance, Antandrus, Ante Aikio, Anthonycaputo7, Antonio "Tony" Montana "Scarface", Antonio Lopez, Aodhdubh, Aparawhatwhat, Applebitemak, Araiderplaya, Arakunem, Aranea Mortem, Arbogastlw, ArglebargleIV, Aris Katsaris, Arjuns4, Armaced, Arthena, Asturianu, Athobbs, Atrix20, Aude, Auntof6, Aurora30, Aus17, AwamerT, BRG, BSveen, Balcer, Bananaluv, Banditnmoi, Barek, Barryob, Bassbasketball03, Bastique, Bbatsell, BeaverWithChainsaw, Becritical, Beepsie, Beland, BenBaker, BenFrantzDale, Bender235, Benjh40, Bentley4, Benwbrum, Berek, Bertilvidet, Bevo74, Bielle, Big iron, Bikasuishin, BilCat, Billy y scout, Bkonrad, Bkwillwm, Bletch, Blood sliver, Blue520, BlueDress28, Bluedogtn, Bobblewik, BobbyLee, Bobo192, Bogey97, Bohanlon, Bomac, Bonadea, Bongwarrior, Bookofsecrets, Borisblue, Boromir123, Bpiereck, Breakingsilly, BrendelSignature, Brian0918, Brianboulton, Brianga, Brianna401, Brighterorange, Brion VIBBER, Brother Officer, Bryan Derksen, Buaidh, Bubbles3, Buck Mulligan, Buddha24, Burntsauce, Burrosman, Butwhatdoiknow, Bvjrm, Byah, C.Fred, C777, CJLL Wright, CMS, CNerd2025, COMPFUNK2, CSWarren, Caliga10, Calliopejen1, Calmypal, Caltas, Calvin 1998, Camron 6, Can't sleep, clown will eat me, Canadian-Bacon, CanadianLinuxUser, Canis Lupus, CapitalR, Capricorn42, CaptQuirk, Captain picard's bald head, Captiannutsack78, Carlaude, CarolGray, Casull, Catgut, Caulde, Cavalier2006, Cburnett, Cchow2, CeltMDC, Ch'marr, Chairman S., Chapmlg, Chargingstar, Charles130, ChaseS08, Chris the speller, ChrisRuvolo, Chrisfortier, Christchurch, Christian List, Chun-hian, Churchmouth00, Chzz, Cinik, Cipherswarm, Circeus, Citation Master, Citicat, CityOfSilver, Civil Engineer III, Clarkbhm, Clorox, Closenplay, Cmc0, Cnewlin, Coastalsteve984, Coasterlover1994, Codyeasyas123, Coffee, Colonies Chris, Cometstyles, CommonsDelinker, Computerdumm1, Conk 9, Conny, Conorblob, Conversion script, Coolcatevan9, CopperSquare, Corpx, Corriebertus, Corusant, Coviepresb1647, Cpl Syx, CrazyC83, Crazymonkey1123, Cribbswh, Croat Canuck, Crobertson, Crunkmasterc, Cs-wolves, CsikosLo, Cst17, CumbiaDude, Cut161, CutOffTies, Cyberguy410, D203, D6, DARTH SIDIOUS 2, DBQer, DBishop1984, DCA Palms, DCEdwards1966, DCUnitedFan2011, DGaw, DIDouglass, DLinth, DMacks, Dabomb87, Daggy174, Dale Arnett, Dale101usa, Dan Hickman, Dan127, DanielCD, Danjel, Danlaycock, Danny, Darkcheese123, Darklilac, Darth Panda, Dave Kennedy, Daven200520, David Justin, Davidcannon, Davidwmanley, DavyJonesLocker, Dayman23, Dayne517, Dbenbenn, Dcarranza, Dcseain, DeadEyeArrow, Deathphoenix, Deborahdotk, Decumanus, Deflective, DennyColt, Deor, DerHexer, Derek.cashman, Dinosaur puppy, Dirtypoolfilms, Disavian, Discospinster, Dispenser, Dkdantastic, Dlaw1979, Dlohcierekim, Dmr2, DocWatson42, Doctor Whom, Dogpop2, Dominus, Don't Feed the Zords, Donchapion38, Dongsauce, Dpowell24486, Dr. Blofeld, DrKiernan, Dragan101, Dryazan, Dtaciuch, Dtoddmiller, Dtracz, Dubyavee, DuckReconMajor, Duoduoduo, Dust Filter, Dvda12345, Dwilso, Dwo, Dygituljunky, Dysepsion, Dysprosia, EEMIV, EJF, EKindig, ESkog, Eagleman484848, EaglesFanInTampa, Ealdgyth, Easleydt8, Ed g2s, Efe, Eivind F Øyangen, El C, Elcobbola, Ellbeecee, Ellywa, Elonka, EncycloPetey, Enviroboy, Epbr123, Epicadam, Epolk, Eric outdoors, Ericamick, Erudecorp, Esanchez7587, Esprit15d, Etan550, Evercat, Everyking, Evice, Excirial, F-402, FF2010, FOX, Fabartus, Fabritzio, Faithlessthewonderboy, Fantrl, Farine, Fasach Nua, Feitclub, Felirenae13, Fieldday-sunday, Fiftytwo thirty, Fingers-of-Pyrex, Firesaw34, Fishing, Fl, Flatterworld, Flayshar, Flewis, Flipperinu, Flowerpotman, Flying fat man, Fnlayson, FoekeNoppert, Folantin, Footballfan190, Forever Dusk, Formida42, Fortunefaded, Fourthords, FrancoGG, Francs2000, FrankCostanza, Freakofnurture, Freddiem, FreplySpang, Friengs4eva, Friginator, Frozenevolution, Fuccccck ypu!, Funnyhat, Furado, Future2008, Fuzheado, Fuzzwhy, GB fan, GUYINOTFAT, Gadfium, Gail, Gammi93, Gdavidp, GeneralEndicott, Gerrish, Gertie1999, GetAMac, Gfoley4, Ghewgill, Gibson4ver, Gilderien, Gillycheesedog, Gimmetrow, Gintar77, Giorgio, Gjd001, Gjs238, Glen, Glennlowney, Gmoney101, Gogo Dodo, Golbez, Good Olfactory, Gracenotes, GraemeMcRae, Graham87, Grammarian2, GrandmaPen, Gravitan, Graywolf323, Green Giant, GregU, Griff12, Griffinofwales, Ground Zero, Gtbob12, Gtstricky, Guanaco, HJ Mitchell, HT1138, Hadal, Haham hanuka, Halmstad, HangingCurve, Happyface666, Hargrimm, Harry Potter, HassourZain, Hdt83, HeckXX, Heff01, HenkvD, Hephaestos, Herecomesthesunking, Hersfold, Hiddenfromview, Highvale, Hiyayaywhopee, Hmains, HokieRNB, Hongooi, Horologium, Hotrodjim, Hrob113, Htgrgwwew, Husond, Hut 8.5, I3illyp, II MusLiM HyBRiD II, INkubusse, Iamdjfloridaman, Ian Moody, Ian Pitchford, IcedNut, Igoldste, Iheartscience13, Illegitimate Barrister, Imjustmatthew, Immunize, Indosauros, Indyfitz, Insanity Incarnate, Inspector 34, Intelati, Invader chris, Iridescent, IronGargoyle, Isis, Isomorphic, Itai, Itsgeneb, J.delanoy, JCO312, JForget, JGKlein, JHunterJ, JIP, JKH-TheReturn, JW1805, Jacobko, Jadtnr1, Jaggerpro, JamesAM, Jamesbrz, Jamesontai, Jamesooders, Jamesward22, Jan eissfeldt, JayJasper, Jaycasper, Jayjg, Jcam, Jcbarr, Jclemens, Jcw69, Jdlambert, Jean-François Clet, Jeepday, Jeff G., Jeffq, Jengod, JensenNR, Jersyko, Jesant13, Jfknrh, Jgolf91, Jhb 10s, Jhendin, Jhortman, Jigesh, JimIrwin, JimWae, Jimmy678910, JinJian, Jivecat, Jkatzen, Jllm06, Jman101, Jmpeagle, Jni, JodyB, Joes a g, John Broughton, John K, John of Reading, John254, JohnBT05, Jojhutton, Jon186, Jorunn, Josemiguelmadrigal, Joseph Solis in Australia, Joshua4, Joshyjenkins, Jpers36, Jshokie1, Jtwoodson, JuJube, Juliancolton, Jultemplet, Jusdafax, Justinep, Jwh, KF, KGasso, KSEltar, Kaeku, Kajasudhakarababu, Kaldari, Kanonkas, Karl2025, Katalaveno, Ke4zz, Keegan, Keilana, KeithH, Ken Gallager, Ken g6, KerenL, Kesac, Kestenbaum, Kevin Myers, Kgenereux, Kgfwright, Khatru2, KikiJones6, Kinaro, Kingcato, Kintetsubuffalo, Kjetil r, Kkgirl21, Klmarcus, KnowledgeOfSelf, Knownfactz, Koavf, Koonoonga, Kooplatroo, Kopaka649, Kostisl, Koyaanis Qatsi, Kozuch, Kpjas, Krich, Kubigula, KuduIO, Kukini, Kumioko, Kungfuadam, Kuru, Kurykh, Kwamikagami, Kwekubo, Kyriosity, L Kensington, L1A1 FAL, L3batman, LGagnon, Landon1980, Landroo, LaotianBoy1991, Laurenrose3091, Law, LeaveSleaves, LedgendGamer, Leebo, Leo53, Leopold Samsonite, Leslie Mateus, LessHeard vanU, Leszek Jańczuk, Leuqarte, Levelistchampion, Levilucas, Levineps, Lhajbox, Liftarn, Lightdarkness, Lightmouse, Lilpinoy 82, Lincolnite, Linusthefish, Little Mountain 5, Livingwords, Llama44, Lobosolo, Locquincer, Loodog, Lookatthis, Loonymonkey, Lovellama, LovesMacs, Loz1992, LtNOWIS, Luckas Blade, Lucky Mitch, Luk, Luna Santin, Lyght, M C Y 1008, MAxImUs ReX, MCruz1984, MECU, MER-C, MJCdetroit, MPD01605, MPF, MacTire02, MacedonianBoy, Mackensen, Madhero88, Maelnuneb, Magister Mathematicae, Magot, MahDingaLing, Mahtanza, Majorly, Malleus Fatuorum, Mandarax, Mani1, Manuel Trujillo Berges, Marauder40, Marek69, Mariya Oktyabrskaya, Mark83, Markhurd, Marlinite, Martin451, MartinDK, MartinRe, MasterOfHisOwnDomain, Materialscientist, Matt Deres, Matthew Yeager, Mattww123456789, Mav, Maximus Rex, Maxis ftw, Mbc362, Mbecker, Mcgotime, MeStevo, Meelar, Melanie K. West, Mememe8595, Menchi, Mermaid from the Baltic Sea, Merotoker1, Methecooldude, Metisgod, Metricmike, Mgturn, Mhsb, MiLo28, Michael Devore, Mike Halterman, Mike Rosoft, Mikeo, Mikeparsnips, Mikevegas40, Mild Bill Hiccup, Milkrocks, Millerlc3, Minesweeper, Miquonranger03, Missraisa, Mistakefinder, Mister Alcohol, Mmoyer, Mobius, Modernist, Moenbro, Mollyb92, Monkeyman, Monkeynoze, Monterey Bay, Morgan Riley, MorrisS, Morrisjbm, Morwen, Mossman93, Moverton, Mr. Haha Jones, Mr. Lefty, Mr.Taka, Mr0grady, MrJanitor1, MrPMonday, Mrscrawford08, Ms2ger, MsDivagin, Mtstroud, Muddfx, MyReference, N419BH, NE2, NEICenergy, NOVAMAN1056, NYyankees51, Nagy, Nakon, Nancy Larcher, Nascar1996, Natalie Erin, NawlinWiki, Nblufire12, Neovu79, NerdyScienceDude, Netalarm, Neurolysis, Neutralhomer, Neverquick, NewEnglandYankee, Nick, Nick C, NigelR, Nihonjoe, Nik 6B, Nikeshoccr, Ninly, Nishkid64, Noah Salzman, Noozgroop, NorCalHistory, North Shoreman, NotAnonymous0, Ntropolis, NuclearWarfare, Num1scot, Nuno

Tavares, Nv8200p, Nycportfolio123, OCNative, Oatmeal batman, Obli, ObtuseAngle, Ochlocrat, Ofscp, Ohnoitsjamie, OlEnglish, Old Guard, Olivier, OllieFury, OmegaPirate89, Omicronpersei8, Omnibus, One, Oneiros, Onepairofpants, Opertinicy, Orange112, Orlady, Ortonmc, Otav347, Owen, Oxymoron83, P64, Painandlove, Paine, Pantothenic, Paradoxian, Paranomia, Parkwells, Patrick, Patrickneil, Patstuart, PaulGS, Paulcmnt, Paulmlieberman, Pavel Vozenilek, Pb30, Pedro, Pekinpekin, PericlesofAthens, Persian Poet Gal, Peter G Werner, Peteturtle, Pethr, Petrichor, Pgk, Pharos, Phil Boswell, PhilKnight, Philip Trueman, PhilipO, Phillies1fan777, Phillip J, Piano non troppo, PierreAbbat, Pinethicket, Pinkadelica, Plange, Plastikspork, Pmanderson, Poikamainentytto, Polynova, Poppop826, Porqin, Possum, Postdlf, Prashanthns, Predater17able, Premiercolleges, Preslethe, Proficient, Proofreader77, Psy guy, Pu483, Punkrawkhighrllr, Punkrocker2021, Pyrospirit, Qqqqqq, Queson, Quinnfabrayrocks411, Quinsareth, Qxz, RA0808, RBrown, RG2, RJHall, RJaguar3, RL0919, RLipstock, RUClimate, Racepacket, Ramblinman1994, Ravedave, Razorflame, Rblaster, Reach Out to the Truth, RebelAt, Reddi, Rentaferret, Repiceman89, Researcher11, Retiono Virginian, RetiredUser2, Retto12, RexNL, Reywas92, Rfc1394, Rgrgyuhui, Rhatsa26X, Rich Farmbrough, Rich257, Richard D. LeCour, Richard75, RichardF, RichardMPT, Rick Block, Rillian, Rjensen, Rjwilmsi, Rlearly, Rljenk, Rmcfan, Roadrunner, Roastytoast, Robert McClenon, Robert86m, RobertG, Robster2001, Roenker, Rogerd, Romanm, Ronhjones, Root Beers, Rornk, RossPatterson, Rrburke, Rreagan007, Rspeer, Rudjek, Rufus843, Ruhrfisch, Rupertslander, Russ3Z, Russ3z, Rutke421, Rvawatch, Ryanaxp, Ryoutou, SJP, SMC, SNIyer12, SPUI, Sallicio, Salvio giuliano, Sam Korn, Sammy Houston, Samuel Blanning, SandyGeorgia, Saopaulo1, Sarah1607, Sardanaphalus, SatyrTN, Sbrown146, ScaldingHotSoup, Scanlan, Sceptre, SchfiftyThree, Scooteristi, Scooterman, Scope creep, Seaphoto, Seb az86556, Serlin, Servant Saber, Seth Ilys, Sexbomb50, Sfmontyo, Shadowjams, Shinpah1, Shocktm, Shoephone1, Shoshonna, Shuldbdoinhw, Sigma419, Signof4, Silverchevy, SimonP, Simpledays, Sjones23, Skillz187, SkipperClipper, Slakr, Slightsmile, Slysplace, Smallbones, Smilesfozwood, Smith03, Snailwalker, Snigbrook, Snowdog, Socially Isolated Hamster, Solicitr, Someguy1221, Son of Eri, Sonoraborealis, Soundoftoday, South Bay, Spawnchild1, Spellmaster, Spitfire, Spydrlink, Srikeit, Starionwolf, StaticGull, StefanieSnag, Steinsky, Stemonitis, Stephen C. Carlson, Stepp-Wulf, StevenL, Stevewonder2, Stillnotelf, Stoli23, Stormie, Strangepalefighter, Student7, StuffOfInterest, Suffusion of Yellow, Sumsum2010, Super burito, Supercoop, Superflyingawesomenerd, Supo1987, Swollib, Syrthiss, Szambo, T r iiss ta, TCO, TDogg310, TLUG, TOttenville8, TUF-KAT, Taco325i, Taka-kun, Takeaway, Takeel, Tanaats, Tap7, Tartarus, Tbhotch, Tdosborne, Tedickey, Teh tennisman, Tellyaddict, Template namespace initialisation script, TenOfAllTrades, TenPoundHammer, Terrymitchell, TexasAndroid, Tgeairn, ThaddeusB, Thatfamousgirl, The Epopt, The High Fin Sperm Whale, The Man in Question, The Obento Musubi, The Punk, The Random Editor, The Singing Badger, The Thing That Should Not Be, The Transhumanist, TheChrisD, TheFossa, TheLakester, Thecheesykid, Themcman1, Themoodyblue, Theornamentalist, Thermal0xidizer, Thermionic1, Thesmothete, Thesouthernhistorian45, Thingg, ThinkBlue, Thomasisthomas, Tide rolls, Tidying Up, Tim Q. Wells, Timmeh, Timneu22, Tiusp, Tmurrayva, Tntjackson, Tnxman307, Tobby72, Tom Morris, TommyBoy, Tomsta576, Tone, Tony Sidaway, Tootiepoll, Tothebarricades.tk, Tpbradbury, Tracer9999, Trimalchio, Tripodero, TuneyLoon, Tuspm, TutterMouse, Twaz, TwinCityIL, Tyw7, UED77, Ufwuct, Ugur Basak, Uiguesalulalu, Ukabia, Ulidia, Ulric1313, Ultraviolet scissor flame, Uncle Dick, Uncle G, UpstateNYer, Uris, Usb10, Usctrojans25, Utcursch, Uva79, Uvaduck, Uvahoops2321, VFHwebdev, Va girl2468, VaGuy1973, Valermos, Valfontis, Van helsing, Vaoverland, Varunner1, Velvetron, Verrai, Versus22, Victor D, Vidiviniwiki, Vildricianus, Vina, Virginialober, Vishnava, VoidBen, Voyagerfan5761, Vpuliva, Vrenator, Vsmith, Vzbs34, WAvegetarian, WODUP, Wackywace, Waggers, WaldoJ, Wapcaplet, Wars, WarthogDemon, WashingtonWillie, Wayne Slam, Wbrayca, Wdfarmer, Weatherman78, Wenli, Wesley J M, West London Dweller, West.andrew.g, WhisperToMe, WikHead, Wiki alf, WikiLaurent, Wikieditor06, Wikiliki, Wikilover000, Wikipediaphile, Wikipelli, Wikiuser100, Wikiz3, Wilhelm Ritter, Will Beback, WillC, William Avery, William Grimes, William Ortiz, Williamb, Wilslove2002, WineSwirl, Wipsenade, Wirticus, Wise, Wizardman, Wizguy5, Wknight94, Wmahan, Woohookitty, WookieInHeat, Woolters, Wooooooot, WoshinidemaXisXback, Wyldephang, XJamRastafire, Xborder14x, Xenlab, Xezbeth, Xwizzardx, Xyzzyva, Yamamoto Ichiro, Yankeefan25306, Yankees76, Yankeyfan315, YellowAssessmentMonkey, YellowMonkey, Yhttyh, Ylem, Yoda789, YolanCh, Yonatan, Youndbuckerz, Youngamerican, ZachPruckowski, ZamorakO o, Zbattgirl, Zeamays, Zidel333, Zimbabweed, Zoe, Zoicon5, Zscout370, Zzyzx11, 2615 anonymous edits

Image Sources, Licenses and Contributors

File:Justice White Official.jpg *Source*: http://en.wikipedia.org/w/index.php?title=File:Justice_White_Official.jpg *License*: unknown *Contributors*: AWeenieMan, Coburnpharr04, Davepape, Jonkerz, Mattrude, 1 anonymous edits

File:Watson-courthouse1.jpg *Source*: http://en.wikipedia.org/w/index.php?title=File:Watson-courthouse1.jpg *License*: unknown *Contributors*: User:Americasroof

File:John Wesley Warrington signature.jpg *Source*: http://en.wikipedia.org/w/index.php?title=File:John_Wesley_Warrington_signature.jpg *License*: unknown *Contributors*: Roseohioresident

File:SupremeCourtofVirginiaBuilding.JPG *Source*: http://en.wikipedia.org/w/index.php?title=File:SupremeCourtofVirginiaBuilding.JPG *License*: unknown *Contributors*: User:Morgan Riley

File:Flag of Virginia.svg *Source*: http://en.wikipedia.org/w/index.php?title=File:Flag_of_Virginia.svg *License*: unknown *Contributors*: ABCD, Awg1010, Dzordzm, Eugenio Hansen, OFS, Fry1989, Homo lupus, Hoodinski, Hoshie, Juiced lemon, Kam Solusar, Kelvinc, Smooth O, Svgalbertian, 12 anonymous edits

File:Flag of the United States.svg *Source*: http://en.wikipedia.org/w/index.php?title=File:Flag_of_the_United_States.svg *License*: unknown *Contributors*: Anomie

File:Seal of Virginia.svg *Source*: http://en.wikipedia.org/w/index.php?title=File:Seal_of_Virginia.svg *License*: unknown *Contributors*: User:Patrickneil

File:Virginia in United States.svg *Source*: http://en.wikipedia.org/w/index.php?title=File:Virginia_in_United_States.svg *License*: unknown *Contributors*: TUBS

Image:Speakerlink.svg *Source*: http://en.wikipedia.org/w/index.php?title=File:Speakerlink.svg *License*: unknown *Contributors*: Woodstone. Original uploader was Woodstone at en.wikipedia

File:Virginia painted relief.png *Source*: http://en.wikipedia.org/w/index.php?title=File:Virginia_painted_relief.png *License*: unknown *Contributors*: User:Patrickneil

File:Shenandoah green.jpg *Source*: http://en.wikipedia.org/w/index.php?title=File:Shenandoah_green.jpg *License*: unknown *Contributors*: Amrinder Arora

File:shenandoah deer 20050521 191017 1.3008x2000.jpg *Source*: http://en.wikipedia.org/w/index.php?title=File:Shenandoah_deer_20050521_191017_1.3008x2000.jpg *License*: unknown *Contributors*: Image copyright 2005 by lorax

File:Pocahontas Saving Life.jpg *Source*: http://en.wikipedia.org/w/index.php?title=File:Pocahontas_Saving_Life.jpg *License*: unknown *Contributors*: Alonzo Chappel

File:Colonial Williamsburg Governors Palace Front Dscn7232.jpg *Source*: http://en.wikipedia.org/w/index.php?title=File:Colonial_Williamsburg_Governors_Palace_Front_Dscn7232.jpg *License*: unknown *Contributors*: Larry Pieniazek

File:Patrick Henry Rothermel.jpg *Source*: http://en.wikipedia.org/w/index.php?title=File:Patrick_Henry_Rothermel.jpg *License*: unknown *Contributors*: w:Peter F. RothermelPeter F. Rothermel (1817–1895)

File:Richmond Civil War ruins.jpg *Source*: http://en.wikipedia.org/w/index.php?title=File:Richmond_Civil_War_ruins.jpg *License*: unknown *Contributors*: War Department. Office of the Chief Signal Officer

File:Virginia Civil Rights Memorial wide.jpg *Source*: http://en.wikipedia.org/w/index.php?title=File:Virginia_Civil_Rights_Memorial_wide.jpg *License*: unknown *Contributors*: Hammersoft, Patrickneil, Sfan00 IMG, Skier Dude, Stifle

File:Norfolk Skyline.jpg *Source*: http://en.wikipedia.org/w/index.php?title=File:Norfolk_Skyline.jpg *License*: unknown *Contributors*: Michael

File:Virginia population map.png *Source*: http://en.wikipedia.org/w/index.php?title=File:Virginia_population_map.png *License*: unknown *Contributors*: Original uploader was Patrickneil at en.wikipedia

File:Christchurchalexandria.jpg *Source*: http://en.wikipedia.org/w/index.php?title=File:Christchurchalexandria.jpg *License*: unknown *Contributors*: User:RebelAt

File:The Pentagon January 2008.jpg *Source*: http://en.wikipedia.org/w/index.php?title=File:The_Pentagon_January_2008.jpg *License*: unknown *Contributors*: David B. Gleason from Chicago, IL

File:Virginia Beach waterfront.jpg *Source*: http://en.wikipedia.org/w/index.php?title=File:Virginia_Beach_waterfront.jpg *License*: unknown *Contributors*: gargola87 from Virginia Beach, VA

File:Colonial Williamsburg ladies.jpg *Source*: http://en.wikipedia.org/w/index.php?title=File:Colonial_Williamsburg_ladies.jpg *License*: unknown *Contributors*: Harvey Barrison from USA

File:Wolf Trap (national park) meadow pavilion.jpg *Source*: http://en.wikipedia.org/w/index.php?title=File:Wolf_Trap_(national_park)_meadow_pavilion.jpg *License*: unknown *Contributors*: User:Gmaxwell

File:Chincoteague pony swim 2007.jpg *Source*: http://en.wikipedia.org/w/index.php?title=File:Chincoteague_pony_swim_2007.jpg *License*: unknown *Contributors*: United States Coast Guard, PA2 Christopher Evanson

File:USA Today building.jpg *Source*: http://en.wikipedia.org/w/index.php?title=File:USA_Today_building.jpg *License*: unknown *Contributors*: User:Patrickneil

File:Rotunda-dusk.jpg *Source*: http://en.wikipedia.org/w/index.php?title=File:Rotunda-dusk.jpg *License*: unknown *Contributors*: Patrickneil, Tdvance

File:A.D. Williams Clinic and West Hospital.jpg *Source*: http://en.wikipedia.org/w/index.php?title=File:A.D._Williams_Clinic_and_West_Hospital.jpg *License*: unknown *Contributors*: Taber Andrew Bain from Richmond, VA, USA

File:Virginia Railway Express train.jpg *Source*: http://en.wikipedia.org/w/index.php?title=File:Virginia_Railway_Express_train.jpg *License*: unknown *Contributors*: John from Southern Maryland, USA

File:Va State Capitol.JPG *Source*: http://en.wikipedia.org/w/index.php?title=File:Va_State_Capitol.JPG *License*: unknown *Contributors*: User:Anderskev

File:Jim Webb Rally.jpg *Source*: http://en.wikipedia.org/w/index.php?title=File:Jim_Webb_Rally.jpg *License*: unknown *Contributors*: Daniel Farrell from Richmond, VA, USA

File:Glennon Hands off to Ore 2007 ECU crop.jpg *Source*: http://en.wikipedia.org/w/index.php?title=File:Glennon_Hands_off_to_Ore_2007_ECU_crop.jpg *License*: unknown *Contributors*: Erich Geist of flickr ()

File:Virginia new sign.jpg *Source*: http://en.wikipedia.org/w/index.php?title=File:Virginia_new_sign.jpg *License*: unknown *Contributors*: Aurora30

MIX
Papier aus verantwortungsvollen Quellen
Paper from responsible sources
FSC® C105338

Printed by Books on Demand GmbH, Norderstedt / Germany